English Language Arts
Units for Grades 9–12

Christopher Shamburg

International Society for Technology in Education
EUGENE, OREGON • WASHINGTON, DC

National Educational Technology Standards for Students Curriculum Series

English Language Arts Units for Grades 9–12

Christopher Shamburg

Director of Book Publishing: *Courtney Burkholder*
Acquisitions Editor: *Jeff V. Bolkan*
Production Editor: *Lynda Gansel*
Production Coordinator: *Maddelyn High*
Graphic Designer: *Signe Landin*
Book Sales and Marketing Manager: *Max Keele*
Copy Editor: *Lynne Ertle*
Indexer: *Pilar Wyman, Wyman Indexing*
Book/Cover Design and Production: *Kim McGovern*

Library of Congress Cataloging-in-Publication Data

Shamburg, Christopher.
  English language arts units for grades 9-12 / Christopher Shamburg.
    p. cm.
  Includes bibliographical references and index.
  ISBN 978-1-56484-240-4 (pbk.)
  1. English language—Study and teaching (Secondary)—United States. 2. Educational technology—
United States.   I. International Society for Technology in Education. II. Title.
  LB1631.S477 2008
  428.0071'2—dc22

                                                        2008005394

First Edition
ISBN: 978-1-56484-240-4

Printed in the United States of America

International Society for Technology in Education (ISTE)
Washington, DC, Office:
    1710 Rhode Island Ave. NW, Suite 900, Washington, DC 20036-3132
Eugene, Oregon, Office:
    175 West Broadway, Suite 300, Eugene, OR 97401-3003
Order Desk: 1.800.336.5191
Order Fax: 1.541.302.3778
Customer Service: orders@iste.org
Book Publishing: books@iste.org
Rights and Permissions: permissions@iste.org
Web: www.iste.org

About ISTE

The International Society for Technology in Education (ISTE) is the trusted source for professional development, knowledge generation, advocacy, and leadership for innovation. A nonprofit membership association, ISTE provides leadership and service to improve teaching, learning, and school leadership by advancing the effective use of technology in PK–12 and teacher education.

Home of the National Educational Technology Standards (NETS), the Center for Applied Research in Educational Technology (CARET), and the National Educational Computing Conference (NECC), ISTE represents more than 85,000 professionals worldwide. We support our members with information, networking opportunities, and guidance as they face the challenge of transforming education. To find out more about these and other ISTE initiatives, visit our Web site at **www.iste.org**.

As part of our mission, ISTE Book Publishing works with experienced educators to develop and produce practical resources for classroom teachers, teacher educators, and technology leaders. Every manuscript we select for publication is carefully peer-reviewed and professionally edited. We look for content that emphasizes the effective use of technology where it can make a difference—increasing the productivity of teachers and administrators; helping students with unique learning styles, abilities, or backgrounds; collecting and using data for decision making at the school and district levels; and creating dynamic, project-based learning environments that engage 21st-century learners. We value your feedback on this book and other ISTE products. E-mail us at **books@iste.org**.

About the Authors

Christopher Shamburg is an associate professor in the Graduate Program in Educational Technology at New Jersey City University. Before teaching college he was a high school English teacher at the Hudson County School of Technology in Jersey City for 10 years and won several awards for his teaching, including Teacher of the Year, a Geraldine R. Dodge Award for Teaching Humanities, a Governor's Award for Outstanding Teaching, and two fellowships from the National Endowment for the Humanities. He has published and presented numerous articles and papers on educational technology and is coauthor of the book *Teachers as Technology Leaders* (ISTE, 2006).

Chris is also a national workshop leader for the Folger Shakespeare Library's Shakespeare Set Free Program and an English teacher for NJeSchool, New Jersey's largest online public high school, where he has developed English courses on podcasting and fanfiction. Chris is a founding member of Radical Teachers—a curriculum development and educational consulting company. He is a highly sought after speaker and workshop leader.

Chris has his BA and MA from Rutgers in English literature and his doctorate in educational technology from Teachers College Columbia University. He lives in Maplewood, New Jersey, with his wife Kate, and two children Luke and Emma. Feel free to contact him at cshamburg@gmail.com or visit www.chrisshamburg.com.

Contributors

Yvette Louis is an assistant professor of English at New Jersey City University. She holds a doctorate from the Department of Comparative Literature at Princeton University and a BA in comparative literature and literature/writing from Columbia University. Her field of specialization is the African Diaspora in the Americas with particular focus on literature written in the United States and the Caribbean in English, Spanish, French, and Dutch. This research incorporates cultural studies, race theory, gender studies, and semiotics. She is currently revising a book project for publication titled "Body Language: The Slave Body and the Word in the Literature of the African Americas."

Kate Mazzetti has her BA in English from Loyola College and her MA in Shakespeare studies from the Shakespeare Institute in Stratford upon Avon, England. She was an English and drama teacher for the Academy of Saint Aloysius in Jersey City, New Jersey, as well as the chairperson of the English Department and director of the Drama Club. She has won several teaching awards including a Geraldine R. Dodge Fellowship Award for New Teachers and a Douglass College Outstanding Teacher Award. She has directed numerous student plays, has extensive experience as an actor and director, and is an alumna of the American Academy of Dramatic Arts.

Jo McLeay is English faculty head at Mater Christi College in Belgrave, Australia, a school of approximately 1,000 girls on the outskirts of Melbourne. She teaches English to students in Years 7–12 and has been teaching for approximately 30 years. Her interests include student-centred learning, and she especially enjoys facilitating literature circles with Year 9 to motivate reading for pleasure. Learning to blog to critically reflect on her work as a teacher and her studies has opened a world of possibilities for professional learning. She has been blogging with students for two years and has become interested in the uses of technology to enhance student learning. Jo is completing her master of education degree, specialising in ICT in education. You can read Jo's blog at http://theopenclassroom.blogspot.com.

Contents

Introduction

I BEGAN TEACHING HIGH SCHOOL ENGLISH in 1991 in a vocational-technical school in Jersey City that was rapidly transforming itself into a high-tech high school. The school had an abundance of technology, an imperative to use it, and very few precedents or guidelines for integrating it in academic disciplines. "How do I effectively teach English with technology?" was a question that consumed me day and night, and I had the resources, latitude, and responsibility to figure it out.

For the next 10 years I researched, pondered, experimented, innovated, failed, and succeeded with technology in the English class. This is how the issue of technology in the high school English class came to dominate my career. I got my doctorate in educational technology with a focus on reflective practice with technology. After teaching high school for 10 years, I began teaching at New Jersey City University's Graduate Program in Educational Technology. It's given me a chance to expand my experiences, research, and conversations with teachers from around the world.

This book originated as the content for my online course Technology in the English Language Arts Curriculum. It's a course I've taught every fall since 2001. I have used various books in the class, but not one of them struck the right balance with practical advice, theory, technology, and grounding in the English class. I developed hundreds of pages of original content for the course, which became the seeds of this book. It's an enterprise that's been 16 years in the making.

This book is organized into three sections: Getting Started, Resource Units, and Appendixes. The chapters in Getting Started will orient you with background information on themes that run throughout the entire book—providing guidance on standards, on conceptions of the English class, on teaching and copyright, and on student research.

The second section consists of the 12 resource units—the focus of the book. Each unit addresses the how, what, and why of the content and methods. This can inform your own professional development as well as guide you in implementing or modifying the ideas with your students. I hope it is part of an important dialogue in reflecting on your own teaching. Each unit provides detailed plans in the following format:

- ISTE NETS for Students and IRA/NCTE Standards
- Keywords
- Objectives
- Unit Description
- Technology
- Supplementary Resources
- Activities
- Assessment

The final section is the Appendixes. Appendixes A and B contain general technical information for using audio and video. Appendix C provides all the handouts referenced in the unit. The handouts are also available in PDF form at www.iste.org/netlan/handouts/.

Please keep in mind that you do not need to have a large budget or be technically savvy to enjoy this book. You will get a lot out it if you have a love of teaching, a curiosity about new methods, and an inclination to believe that digital technologies can reshape and re-energize the high school English class.

Clarifications

Here are some clarifications about the English classroom and technology that this book addresses. The misconceptions are in bold followed by clarifications based on my work during the last 16 years.

Students are more media-savvy than their teachers. Some students may be technically proficient and knowledgeable, but the vast majority of them often lack the judgment and discretion to evaluate and use media effectively. They need a broader and deeper understanding of power structures, history, culture, and literacy—a context that English teachers can provide.

Plagiarism is a major problem when giving student research projects. Many research projects do not capitalize on today's information technology or students' interests and burgeoning skills. Teachers can develop compelling projects that teach meaningful skills that most students can't or won't plagiarize.

Students are bored by the great books. Great stories, interesting characters, and beautiful language are intrinsically interesting to people of all ages. Students need to be scaffolded in unfamiliar media (e.g., long novels or Shakespearean drama) with techniques that engage them and involve them in the works.

When using Web sources, get your information from "credible sources." You need to look at the domain name (.com or .org, for example) and can trust mainstream sources such as CNN and *The New York Times*. We have to take a hard look at our criteria for credibility and the shelf life for trust. When we got our news from three networks and the major newspapers, watchdogs would remind us that "all news is views." The sense of this warning is even more relevant in the Digital Age. We have to teach students to detect bias, credibility, expertise, and authority in all sources.

Books are passé to students. The book as a technical invention is almost unsurpassable— durable, low cost, about 3 MB of ROM, capable of 20 megapixel images with better text resolution than any other desktop or portable device (including high-definition television). Books are the ultimate distance learning technology—having the ability to transport an individual into the life, times, relationships, and thoughts of another human being.

The high school English class should focus on books—media resources are for the art or social studies class. Language is inextricably linked to many forms of communication. Look at the world around us and your own experiences. Where do you get information? What do you read? Undoubtedly, the English language has become a multimedia experience.

Reading is less important in the Digital Age. Perhaps never before in human history has reading been more important. Volumes of text can come to you from anywhere in the world in a matter of seconds. Text-based e-mail is a basic form of communication that is immediate and permanent. Text is ubiquitous—hyperlinked, scrolling, tagged to images, and integrated in video.

Language arts teachers should embrace the theory of multiple intelligences and interdisciplinary study. The theory of multiple intelligences and interdisciplinary study are extremely valuable if applied thoughtfully. However, making the Globe Theatre out of Popsicle sticks or creating a PowerPoint presentation on the Spanish Armada is not the same as giving students a meaningful appreciation of Shakespeare. Multidisciplinary units and the theory of multiple intelligences have often been used as a distraction from doing the work of high school English.

The possibilities of using technology in the language arts class are limitless. There are limits. Advanced uses of technology do not translate to advanced skills in English class. Enthusiastically embracing a complex or time-consuming technology in the English class can be misguided.

You need the latest technology and a computer lab to take advantage of the ideas in this book. Actually, teaching language arts in a computer lab can be counterproductive. Most of the ideas in this book can be accomplished with two to three computers in a classroom. These ideas do not require expensive software or hardware.

High School English teachers can be conservative and resistant to technology. High school English teachers are usually the most innovative, thoughtful, and reflective educators in a school. Furthermore, after parents, teachers hold the most responsibility for a student's education. Teachers need to be skeptical of fads, trends, and the uninformed decisions of administrators, outside experts, politicians, and other interest groups.

Students are more motivated to learn when they use technology. Technology itself is not a motivating factor. In fact, used indiscriminately, it can quash a student's interest and impede meaningful learning.

Teachers need to know the books, plays, and technologies inside and out before they use them with students. Part of your objective is guiding yourself and students in mutual discovery. Navigating your students though new material, troubling technical problems, and ambiguous content will lead to a richer experience for you and them.

As you read this book and learn more about me in the process, I hope you get the impression that I would like you to agree with these clarifications. I also hope you get the impression that I would also like it if you *disagreed* with some of them. Please send me an e-mail (cshamburg@gmail.com) if you have any better ideas.

Values and the Hidden Curriculum

This book is about values as well as technology. We send powerful and unspoken messages about our values to students through the methods we use in our classrooms. This is often referred to as the hidden curriculum. With the hidden curriculum, actions speak louder (and in some cases contrary to) the words we use to profess our values. With this in mind, I'd like to point out the values that run throughout the units of this book. They might not be articulated to your students, but keep in them in mind as you read the units.

The first message is about the value of students. All of these units validate student experiences and interests. These activities send the message that "your ideas and interests are important." As students articulate their experiences in activities such as blogging, movie making, or memoir writing, classrooms should nurture and empower students' interests, initiative, interpretations, and creativity.

The hidden curriculum of these units also places a value on participation—in culture, society, and politics. History and literature are not disconnected or distant experiences and culture is not an exclusive club. In most of these units, students become active participants in culture, politics, and society—whether podcasting to the world or appropriating existing stories and creating original fanfiction from them. It is common to hear about hands-on math and hands-on science in schools. These units are about hands-on culture—culture that includes Shakespeare and YouTube.

Another value conveyed in the hidden curriculum of these units is authenticity. These activities are not decontexualized experiences or part of the "game of school," a game with its own set of rules and rewards unconnected to the outside world. The majority of these units give students a direct connection to engaging, real-life activities. All of the units embody John Dewey's charge that "Education is not preparation for life, but life itself."

These units demonstrate the value of community. Students are scaffolded in ways to respect the work of their classmates as well as to intelligently connect to the world at large. This value is based on the reality of our networked world as well as on the paradox that learning more about yourself as an individual involves engaging in networks and communities of other people. The units on wikis, fanfiction, and online video saliently embody this value of community.

Finally, these units convey the value of reflection. Every unit begins with a compelling reason for the importance of the skills, technologies, and objectives. The procedures for each unit acknowledge the realities and importance of work done in the classroom.

Words in Action

A good way to succinctly capture the theme of this book is to say that the high school English class should be a place for words in *action* and words in *actions*. To paraphrase Paulo Freire, literacy is about engaging with the word and the world. This book offers a holistic approach to using technology in the high school English class—an approach that runs counter to the sight of students sitting quietly in neat rows, silently typing at computers with headphones on.

Technology in the English class is not about connecting students to computers, but about intelligently connecting students to the world and getting them to learn more about themselves and the world in the process.

Words in action compel us to excitedly read a story or play, are meaningfully linked in hypertext, or act as the narration of a podcast or a student video. They can be part of a persuasive public speech, make up the dialogue of a film, or accompany the movements of a character in a play. They can organize a rally or start an enterprise of great pitch from an idea. Language arts education is about developing the power of words—words that are spoken, linked, recorded, written, shouted, enacted—for different audiences and with different media—from digital video to the vibrations in the air.

The ideas in this book value nonprint literacies and coding systems, but also acknowledge that language—the coding system of words—is more important in the Digital Age than at any other time.

SECTION 1

Getting Started

CHAPTER 1

Standards

THE UNITS IN THIS BOOK are guided by and correlated with the two major sets of standards that relate to the high school English teacher: the National Educational Technology Standards for Students (NETS•S), developed by ISTE in 1998 and refined in 2007, and the Standards for the English Language Arts, created in 1996 by the International Reading Association (IRA) and the National Council of Teachers of English (NCTE). These standards complement each other and can jointly inform English teachers in the content and methods of their work. They represent the collective wisdom that these national organizations are in unique positions to aggregate, organize, and disseminate. Standards offer a way to improve the education of our students; they do, however, need to be applied thoughtfully.

I would like to share a cautionary tale about standards. I was recently invited to talk to a group of language arts teachers from a large school district on the applications of technology. I began by rhetorically asking, "What does it mean to be literate today?" Several of the teachers began to repeat the skills listed in the state's curriculum content standards. When I pressed them to go beyond this definition, more teachers elaborated points from the state document. The district department chair sat nearby with a look of contentment, gleefully adding that "my teachers know their standards." As I tried to get them to relate these standards to their own ideas, experiences, and practice, the group grew increasingly silent. This encounter was disturbing to me. What I expected was a conversation that linked the idea of literacy to their experiences and observations—connecting the changes in the world to what happens in classrooms. It made me wonder how deeply teachers are actually reflecting on and investing themselves in fundamental questions regarding literacy, technology, and the future of language arts. Were the state standards precluding the conversations, debates, and personal reflections that help teachers grow?

We create a reductionist trap when we limit the complexities of teaching and learning to a set of standards—diminishing our teaching to an authoritative list of inputs and outputs. This can have a detrimental effect on our profession and in our classrooms. In discussing possible problems with national language arts standards before the IRA/NCTE standards were released, Don Zancanella (1994) points to the potential of standards to freeze the subject-matter curriculum and to stifle school and classroom innovation. Too often, those who criticize national standards are marginalized as provincial or as apologists for low expectations. However, we as educators should never abdicate our rights to reflect on, judge, analyze, and debate national and state standards. As the recent revision of the ISTE NETS•S indicates, standards are not static dictates, but guidelines that evolve as a result of events and pressures in the changing world.

The oldest and first definition of *standard* in the *Oxford English Dictionary* (1989) includes a "conspicuous object, raised on a pole to indicate the rallying-point of an army" (n.p.). We should look at the standards as rallying points that represent a consensus of the priorities of researchers, experts, and practitioners. They highlight the landscape of our profession but are also subject to our own interpretations, resources, and local conditions. I am convinced that national standards have the potential to raise student performance and improve education, but they should also bring us into local and national dialogues as invested stakeholders in the values they represent.

National Educational Technology Standards for Students

The NETS Project originated to "enable stakeholders in PreK–12 education to develop national standards for the educational uses of technology that will facilitate school improvement in the United States" (ISTE, 1998, p. 3). From the NETS Project, the NETS•S were developed in 1998. The NETS•S were revised in June of 2007 with a recognition of the need to make standards applicable and accessible to teachers and students around the world, and indeed, the NETS•S are used in every U.S. state and in many countries (ISTE, 2007). In an interview for *District Administration*, Don Knezek, the CEO of ISTE, attributes the revisions to globalization, developments in technology, and "pressures from the flattening world and the slippage in our nation's leadership in innovation and in its world economic leadership" (Stager, 2007, n.p.). The 2007 ISTE NETS•S are:

1. **Creativity and Innovation**

    Students demonstrate creative thinking, construct knowledge, and develop innovative products and processes using technology. Students:

    a. apply existing knowledge to generate new ideas, products, or processes

    b. create original works as a means of personal or group expression

    c. use models and simulations to explore complex systems and issues

    d. identify trends and forecast possibilities

2. **Communication and Collaboration**

   Students use digital media and environments to communicate and work collaboratively, including at a distance, to support individual learning and contribute to the learning of others. Students:

   a. interact, collaborate, and publish with peers, experts, or others employing a variety of digital environments and media

   b. communicate information and ideas effectively to multiple audiences using a variety of media and formats

   c. develop cultural understanding and global awareness by engaging with learners of other cultures

   d. contribute to project teams to produce original works or solve problems

3. **Research and Information Fluency**

   Students apply digital tools to gather, evaluate, and use information. Students:

   a. plan strategies to guide inquiry

   b. locate, organize, analyze, evaluate, synthesize, and ethically use information from a variety of sources and media

   c. evaluate and select information sources and digital tools based on the appropriateness to specific tasks

   d. process data and report results

4. **Critical Thinking, Problem Solving, and Decision Making**

   Students use critical thinking skills to plan and conduct research, manage projects, solve problems, and make informed decisions using appropriate digital tools and resources. Students:

   a. identify and define authentic problems and significant questions for investigation

   b. plan and manage activities to develop a solution or complete a project

   c. collect and analyze data to identify solutions and/or make informed decisions

   d. use multiple processes and diverse perspectives to explore alternative solutions

5. **Digital Citizenship**

   Students understand human, cultural, and societal issues related to technology and practice legal and ethical behavior. Students:

   a. advocate and practice safe, legal, and responsible use of information and technology

   b. exhibit a positive attitude toward using technology that supports collaboration, learning, and productivity

   c. demonstrate personal responsibility for lifelong learning

   d. exhibit leadership for digital citizenship

6. Technology Operations and Concepts

Students demonstrate a sound understanding of technology concepts, systems, and operations. Students:

a. understand and use technology systems

b. select and use applications effectively and productively

c. troubleshoot systems and applications

d. transfer current knowledge to learning of new technologies

Standards for the English Language Arts

In 1996, the IRA and the NCTE—the two leading organizations for language arts teachers—partnered and introduced Standards for the English Language Arts. Of these 12 standards, four (1, 6, 7, and 8) directly address technology and nonprint texts; however, all 12 standards are addressed in this book and can be meaningfully integrated with technology.

The rationale for addressing technology in the IRA/NCTE standards is summed up in the joint statement that "electronic technologies, perhaps more than any other recent innovation, have heightened our sense of the need for reform and have raised our expectations of what students must know and be able to do in the English language arts" (IRA/NCTE, 1996, pp. 40–41). These standards have guided the development of state standards and curriculum frameworks over the last decade. The IRA/NCTE standards are:

1. Students read a wide range of print and non-print texts to build an understanding of texts, of themselves, and of the cultures of the United States and the world; to acquire new information; to respond to the needs and demands of society and the workplace; and for personal fulfillment. Among these texts are fiction and nonfiction, classic, and contemporary works.

2. Students read a wide range of literature from many periods in many genres to build an understanding of the many dimensions (e.g., philosophical, ethical, aesthetic) of human experience.

3. Students apply a wide range of strategies to comprehend, interpret, evaluate, and appreciate texts. They draw on their prior experience, their interactions with other readers and writers, their knowledge of word meaning and of other texts, their word identification strategies, and their understanding of textual features (e.g., sound-letter correspondence, sentence structure, context, graphics).

4. Students adjust their use of spoken, written, and visual language (e.g., conventions, style, vocabulary) to communicate effectively with a variety of audiences and for different purposes.

5. Students employ a wide range of strategies as they write and use different writing process elements appropriately to communicate with different audiences for a variety of purposes.

6. Students apply knowledge of language structure, language conventions (e.g., spelling and punctuation), media techniques, figurative language, and genre to create, critique, and discuss print and nonprint texts.

7. Students conduct research on issues and interests by generating ideas and questions, and by posing problems. They gather, evaluate, and synthesize data from a variety of sources (e.g., print and nonprint texts, artifacts, people) to communicate their discoveries in ways that suit their purpose and audience.

8. Students use a variety of technological and information resources (e.g., libraries, databases, computer networks, video) to gather and synthesize information and to create and communicate knowledge.

9. Students develop an understanding of and respect for diversity in language use, patterns, and dialects across cultures, ethnic groups, geographic regions, and social roles.

10. Students whose first language is not English make use of their first language to develop competency in the English language arts and to develop understanding of content across the curriculum.

11. Students participate as knowledgeable, reflective, creative, and critical members of a variety of literacy communities.

12. Students use spoken, written, and visual language to accomplish their own purposes (e.g., for learning, enjoyment, persuasion, and the exchange of information).

Standards for the English Language Arts © 1996 by the International Reading Association and the National Council of Teachers of English.

Guidelines for Composing with Nonprint Media

Of particular interest is the continued work in the field of new literacies and nonprint texts done by NCTE. This focus is captured in NCTE's (2003) position statement "On Composing with Nonprint Media," which resolves that the NCTE will do the following:

- encourage preservice, inservice, and staff development programs that will focus on new literacies, multimedia composition, and a broadened concept of literacy;

- encourage research and develop models of district, school, and classroom policies that would promote multimedia composition;

- encourage integrating multimedia composition in English language arts curriculum and teacher education, and in refining related standards at local, state, and national levels; and

- renew the commitment expressed in the 1983 Resolution on Computers in English and Language Arts to achieve equity of access to the full range of composing technologies. (n.p.)

This resolution acknowledges that we are living in a world that is "increasingly nonprint-centric" and that literacy in these nonprint texts is a responsibility of the English teacher. The ideas in this book address new literacies, supported by the collective guidance of the NETS•S and IRA/NCTE standards.

Both sets of standards offer important guidance for high school English teachers. In short, the IRA/NCTE standards offer a compelling portrait of what it means to be literate in the Information Age, and the NETS•S offer a comprehensive and structured view of the technological knowledge, skills, and mindsets that characterize a productive, connected, and engaged citizen of the early 21st century.

Works Cited

International Reading Association (IRA) & National Council of Teachers of English (NCTE). (1996). *Standards for the English language arts*. United States: Author.

International Society for Technology in Education (ISTE). (1998). *National educational technology standards for students*. Eugene, OR: Author. Also available online at http://cnets.iste.org/students/s_standards./html

International Society for Technology in Education (ISTE). (2007). *National educational technology standards for students* (2nd ed.). Eugene, OR: Author. Also available online at www.iste.org/Content/NavigationMenu/NETS/For_Students/NETS_Students.htm

National Council of Teachers of English (NCTE). (2003). *On composing with nonprint media*. Retrieved August 1, 2007, from www.ncte.org/about/over/positions/category/comp/114919.htm

Oxford English Dictionary (2nd ed.). (1989). Oxford University Press. Retrieved from http://dictionary.oed.com

Stager, G. (2007, June). Refreshing the ISTE technology standards. *District Administration*. Retrieved June 21, 2007, from www.districtadministration.com/viewarticle.aspx?articleid=1186

Zancanella, D. (1994). Local conversations, national standards, and the future of English. *The English Journal, 83*(3), 23–29.

CHAPTER **2**

Reflecting on the High School English Class

OUR ASSUMPTIONS about the nature of the high school English class powerfully affect our work in the classroom. However, these assumptions are often unarticulated or under-examined. In my work as a high school English teacher and teacher educator, taking a broader view of the high school English class has helped sharpen my vision about what could and should happen there. This broader view involves engaging in dialogues with other teachers; questioning preconceptions; conducting research into the history of education; and reflecting on what, why, and how we work in our classrooms.

The High-School-English-Teacher Thing to Do

When I first started teaching high school English I was at our district's holiday party talking to my superintendent, a man with a very progressive view of education. As I was describing the work I was doing with *The Scarlet Letter* in my American Literature course, he interrupted me and asked why I was teaching that book. I stammered up some comments about "the importance of the book in literary history," but I was really stumped. What an important and simple question—and I didn't have an adequate answer. Although my initial reaction was to dismiss him as uninformed on how high school English classes work (with my year and a half of experience under my belt), I knew that the conversation had revealed a major fault line in my work. I should be able to explain why I teach what I teach (at least enough to convince myself). Indeed, there are many good reasons to teach *The Scarlet Letter*. I just didn't have any.

At the time, teaching that book seemed to me like the "high-school-English-teacher thing to do," a reason that was eventually unsatisfying. In fact, many of my actions—teaching the five-paragraph essay and leading discussions on the light and dark imagery in *Romeo and Juliet*—were done because they seemed like the high-school-English-teacher thing to do. I had a preconceived idea—based on my own experiences as a student and from movies and TV shows—of what happens in the English class. I had a mental composite of the high school English teacher, and my job was now to fit into it. Who needed standards, national organizations, deep reflections, readings, and research when the archetype of the high school English teacher was so easily available? When I began to go beyond this preconception, my best teaching—with and without technology—happened.

Fundamental questions about why and what is taught can simmer below the surface of our daily activities as teachers. Addressing questions about the context, content, and purpose of high school English can help inform our decisions and methods. What is the high school English class, and what is supposed to happen there? What is the role of technology in modern literacy? How and why should we teach fiction? What are the best ways to teach writing and why?

Barriers to Reflection

English teachers have distinct disadvantages when trying to engage in this type of reflection. For many, this type of reflection can seem like a luxury with the excessive amount of duties English teachers have—reading the books and plays that get taught, grading student papers and essays, preparing students for the SAT and other high-stakes tests, reviewing students' college essays, satisfying an inordinate number of requests for college recommendations, and often setting the standards for writing for the entire school. (I would also add numbering paperback books and tracking down the students who don't return them—a seemingly trivial but time-consuming job.)

The importance of the high school English teacher's job to prepare literate adults contributes to a resistance to reflection as well. Students come to high school as 14-year-old kids and leave as adults—able to vote, go to college, and join the military. Many of the skills relating to college, work, and participation in society and culture are taught in the English class. It is this awesome responsibly that can discourage change because nobody wants to get it wrong, and changes can be wrong. In their book *Teaching with Technology*, Sandholtz, Ringstaff, and Dwyer (1997) write, "Teachers enter the profession with deeply held notions about how to conduct school. If these beliefs are commonly held and help teachers negotiate the uncertainty of work in schools, no wonder teachers are reticent to adopt practices that have not stood the test of time" (p. 36).

A related factor that discourages reflection is the special place the English teacher has in our collective consciousness. Our fascination with the high school English teacher is demonstrated by the popularity of the job in books, movies, and TV shows. It seems to be the most popularly depicted educator in mass media and a figure that most people have a preconceived notion about, for better or worse. Most English teachers enter the classroom with some conception of their professional selves based on movies such as *Dead Poets Society, Freedom*

Writers, *Up the Down Staircase*, or *Dangerous Minds* as well as the powerful influence of their own experiences in years of English classes.

While images of clueless, dictatorial, or pedantic teachers abound in the media, I have found it paradoxical that even (and especially?) images of dynamic and liberating figures—from Hilary Swank in *Freedom Writers* to Robin Williams in *Dead Poets Society*—eventually leave me with a wistful feeling. Reflecting on my own teaching and view of these movies, I can't help but think that the inability to duplicate their successes or a fundamental mismatch in teaching styles left me somewhat deflated. These movies often present a teacher with a powerful and unique teaching style that inspires emulation, not the deep professional reflection that can substantively improve our practice from the inside out.

My point in describing these inhibitions to reflective practice is not to portray English teachers as inert. My experience has been quite the contrary. English teachers I've seen and worked with were some of the most dynamic and creative forces in education. However, my point is that English teachers should reexamine the context of their work, that the construct of the high school English class needs to be reconceptualized. Many teachers do a great job of not just giving their students "the fish" so they will eat for the day, but teaching them "how to fish" so they will eat for a lifetime. My work is to help teachers and students find new ponds with bigger fish.

Not Even Past

A character in William Faulkner's *Requiem for a Nun* says, "The past is not dead. In fact, it's not even past." This quote is loaded with meaning for the high school English teacher. It's important to keep in mind that the high school English class does not have a long past compared with subjects such as math and science, nor was it conceived with the type of forethought that matches its power on our lives. Considering the place it has in our professional and cultural consciousness, it is hard to believe that the high school English class is barely 100 years old. The subject was formalized by the National Education Association's Committee of Ten in 1894, and built on the early attempts to legitimize the study of English literature at high schools and colleges and prepare students for the literature on college entrance exams.

The ghosts of the Committee of Ten still haunt us today. A hallmark of the committee's work was the eventual development of a single curriculum for both the college bound and those going directly into the workforce for a new industrial society (Kliebard, 2004, pp. 6–11). For the English class, this meant the study of literature as well as practical skills needed for the early 20th century. Their vision of the high school English class has survived remarkably well. Writing about the committee's design of the high school English class, Ben Nelms (2000, p. 49), the former editor of *The English Journal*, writes that "the extent to which the subject they invented still stands, in virtually the same form … is dramatic testimony to the success of their efforts." The problem is that college entrance exams no longer test for literature and that students need 21st-century Information Age skills, not 20th-century Industrial Age skills.

Future Directions

Major overhauls of the subject have been proposed, and quite persuasively. Some mainstream reformers have argued for a dramatic shift in the subject's focus, and a total reformation of schools and schooling is a plausible direction, even one in which the current subject is eliminated. In the issue of *The English Journal* celebrating the centennial of high school English (March 1994), Robert Yagelski's article, "Literature and Literacy: Rethinking English as a School Subject," starkly contrasts ways that language is used outside the classroom with ways that language is taught inside the classroom. Yagelski reflects that "It no longer worries me much that so many high school students don't seem able to write effective essays of literary analysis. What worries me is that we ask them so often to do so" (p. 30). Many reformers offer a more radical vision. In *Horace's School: Redesigning the American High School* (1992), the education theorist Theodore Sizer offers an interdisciplinary model of the reformed high school, a model that eliminates the English teacher and redistributes the responsibilities to generalists and history-philosophy teachers.

Despite the pressures, expectations, and conflicts, an illuminating perspective on what should happen in the English class comes when we broadly look at how narrative, communication, and language are practiced today *outside* of schools. Many of these uses are tied to an increasing array of communication media and the growing ability to work with technologies that were previously available only to professionals in the media industry. People can create videos with cell phones and post them on YouTube for millions to view and react to. Kids read a Harry Potter book and then write and critique sequels to the story on the Internet. A writer can become a national political force with compelling ideas and a free blog account. Families stay in daily contact from around the world through e-mail and photo-sharing Web sites. Resources, content, and news stories are created, reviewed, rated, and shared *by* users and *for* users through tags and social software sites. These are just a few examples of how converging technologies are shaping society to give individuals more control and participation. People can create compelling content and connect to each other without the filters and interference previously associated with worldwide access.

We need to be thinking on a grand scale, exploring the effect that writing had on the Greeks and the printing press had on the early modern Europeans. As civilizations incorporated writing and then print into daily life, their skills, thoughts, mental schemas, and world views radically shifted, and the world saw the evolution of philosophy, the rise of cities, and the blossom of renaissance movements. High school English teachers now have an opportunity and a responsibility to fundamentally reconceptualize our missions and recast how and what we do in the Digital Age.

New Literacies

An idea that can us help navigate these changes in school is the concept of *new literacies*. The work in the field of new literacies intertwines social, cognitive, political, and technological development. The idea of new literacies involves skillfully working with the array of communication technology available today; expanding our ideas about schooling to connect more with the world; and facilitating social, economic, and political activity with these new skills

(Gee, 2004; Kist, 2005; Lankshear & Knobel, 2003). It stems from the work of Paulo Freire, who taught literacy as working with the word and the world.

I am not highlighting new literacies to give teachers another piece of jargon, but as a schema to organize the myriad of "literacies" that they seem to be responsible for. One of the more daunting pressures of the high school English teacher is keep track of all of the "literacies" that seem to relate to the English class—information literacy, cultural literacy, visual literacy, media literacy, multiple literacies, technological literacies, and 21st-century literacies. All of these literacies have persuasive proponents and each have their priorities and agendas. Using the ideas of new literacies can be a lens and a guide to inform your work in the classroom.

Innovation and Technology

There are some interesting comparisons between developing ways to use media technologies and discovering methods for teaching with technologies. Media analysts and historians have long noted that new media creators initially adopt the content and style of their predecessors. For example, many early films were shot with a stationary camera in front of a stage play, without much consideration for the attributes of the new medium. Filmmakers eventually developed a unique language with close-ups, montages, panning, and zooms. Similarly, teachers initially fold technologies into their existing ideas of teaching. Eventually, however, teachers can find new methods, goals, and languages for these technologies in our practice.

Various models of teachers' use of technology capture this adaptation to innovation (Hooper & Rieber, 1995; Sandholtz, Ringstaff, & Dwyer, 1997). Teachers start by using a new technology in their existing practice and can eventually become not just an innovative user, but an innovative educator; they begin zooming and panning in their practice.

The goal of this chapter was to challenge some of the popular notions concerning limitations in the high school English class, and, in turn, encourage a fresh perspective on the work of high school English teachers. Looking at our assumptions, the history of the subject, suggestions for reform, and how language is practiced outside of schools gives us a wider context to consider innovation with technology.

Works Cited

Gee, J. P. (2004). *Situated language and learning: A critique of traditional schooling.* New York: Routledge.

Hooper, S., & Rieber, L. P. (1995). Teaching with technology. In A. C. Ornstein (Ed.), *Teaching: Theory into practice* (pp. 154–170). Needham Heights, MA: Allyn and Bacon.

Kist, W. (2005). *New literacies in action: Teaching and learning in multiple media.* New York: Teachers College Press.

Kliebard, H. (2004). *The struggle for the American curriculum, 1893–1958.* New York: Routledge.

Lankshear, C., & Knobel, M. (2003). *New literacies: Changing knowledge and classroom learning.* Buckingham, UK: Open University Press.

Nelms, B. (2000, January). Reconstructing English: From the 1890s to the 1990s and beyond. *The English Journal, 89*(3), 49–59.

Sandholtz, J. H., Ringstaff, C., & Dwyer, D. C. (1997). *Teaching with technology: Creating student-centered classrooms.* New York: Teachers College Press.

Sizer, T. (1992). *Horace's school: Redesigning the American high school.* Boston: Houghton Mifflin.

Yagelski, R. (1994, March). Literature and literacy: Rethinking English as a school subject. *The English Journal, 83*(3), 23–29.

CHAPTER 3

Copyright, Digital Media, and Teaching High School English

THE IDEAS IN THIS BOOK and trends in technology and in education involve integrating original and existing media. In digital environments, students simultaneously become content consumers and content creators. With educational practices involving remixes, edits, and mashups and the availability of images, text, and audio on the Web, it is imperative that students become ethical users of intellectual property. The absence of this knowledge can lead to illegal uses and unethical habits, or can have a chilling effect by intimidating teachers into avoiding the use of digital media. This chapter takes a thoughtful and comprehensive look at copyright, digital media, and the high school English class.

What Is Copyright?

Copyrights, trademarks, and patents are three legal ways that intellectual properties are protected, but copyright has the biggest effect on the day-to-day work of most English teachers. Copyright begins once an idea is expressed in a fixed form—a printed document, an e-mail message, a recorded song. Your lessons, your students' essays, and Eminem's music are all equally protected by copyright. Copyright gives the creator exclusive rights to reproduce, make derivative works, or perform his or her material. Copyright does not apply to ideas, only to the expression of ideas. Copyright is automatic; you do not need to attach the © symbol or register your work.

Ms. Mulvahill's Dilemma

Ms. Mulvahill's students are creating a podcast radio show for their journalism class. They are creating features on sports, arts, culture, and current events. Several students have done exemplary work, mixing contemporary music with their original reports and essays. Ms. Mulvahill believes that the use of audio recordings, ripped from CDs and downloaded from iTunes, is completely legal for use by her students in her class under the fair use guidelines—legal guidelines for the unauthorized reproduction of copyrighted print, music, and video material. However, several students want to put their work on the school's Web site, another student wants to put it on his MySpace page, and one student wants to submit it to a local radio station. Although she is buoyed by the students' enthusiasm, she realizes that the power to invoke fair use for education diminishes as work is duplicated and shared outside the classroom.

She discusses copyright law with the students, emphasizing the freedoms of fair use and the fact that the law protects their work just as it does the products of major recording artists. Several students request the rights to use the original music; they write to the record labels that hold the copyrights to the music and carefully explain what they have done and what they want to do with the music. All of the students receive stern letters forbidding them to continue. What can she do?

Copyright protections do not last indefinitely. However, laws have changed over the years, and there is no single time period for the protection of all material. For works created after January 1, 1978, copyright extends to 70 years after the author's death. Different copyright time periods are allotted for works for hire, works before 1978, and unpublished works before 1978. When a copyright is over, the work passes into the public domain—free to be copied, published, manipulated, or printed by anyone. In addition, the creator of a work can choose to put his or her work in the public domain, or a work could be authored by the U.S. government and not eligible for copyright protection. For a comprehensive description of a copyright holder's rights and a list of time limitations of copyrighted material, see *Copyright Basics*, authored by the U.S. Copyright Office (2000, www.copyright.gov/circs/circ1.html).

Fair Use

While the U.S. Constitution gives Congress the right to establish copyright law, the legal principle of fair use allows for the unauthorized use of copyrighted materials. Fair use is an extremely valuable tool for educators. Although codified into law in 1976, fair use has a legal history in the United States that goes back to the 18th century. Fair use allows educators and others to make reasonable amounts of copies without seeking the copyright holder's permission based on four interrelated factors. The factors are:

1. The purpose and character of the use

2. The nature of the copyrighted work

3. The amount and substantiality of the portion taken

4. The effect of the use upon the potential market

A consideration of the purpose and character of the use gives leeway for educational purposes—as well as those involving satire, criticism, and commentary. For example, a parody of a song, a clip used in a movie review, or a quote of a book in a literary review can all fall within fair use. The character of the use also refers to factors such as the planning and reach of the copying. For example, last-minute or impromptu copying is more acceptable than copying that is part of a school policy. The nature of the material is also a factor. In general, it is more permissible to copy factual material—like a weather report—than more creative works. Likewise, it is more permissible to copy smaller amounts than larger amounts. Finally, the degree to which your copying hurts the market of the copyright holder is considered. For a deep and balanced look at fair use, see the University of Texas's *Fair Use of Copyrighted Materials* (2005, www.utsystem.edu/OGC/intellectualProperty/copypol2.htm) and Stanford University's *Copyright and Fair Use* (2005, http://fairuse.stanford.edu).

Fair use is an important ally to teachers and there is an especially important legal argument for school use: the "good faith fair use defense." Steven McDonald (2004), a lawyer specializing in copyright law, sums it up.

> In terms of risk analysis, the "good faith fair use defense" (17 U.S.C. 504(c)(2)) provides a potent defense for nonprofit educational institutions and libraries that simply make an honest mistake when trying to interpret the vast gray area of fair use—no statutory damages can be awarded. In fact, the mere existence of that defense probably makes it considerably less likely that they would even be defendants in the first place. (n.p.)

If you are familiar with the fair use guidelines and believe your use fits, then you have a great deal of protection.

More on Ms. Mulvahill

Ms. Mulvahill's class was working within fair use when she allowed students to use copyrighted music in their projects. Even if a record company believed that she was not, it would be difficult for them to take any serious legal action against her because of the good faith defense. They might be more inclined to do something (and more successful in pressing their case) if their music was being broadcast on the Internet by kids, as it could damage record sales. Ms. Mulvahill does realize that broadcasting the content on the Web seems beyond fair use, and she is very interested in developing ethical standards for her class and her students.

Some Misconceptions about Fair Use

At the time fair use was codified in 1976, the ambiguity of the four factors was a great concern for music and print publishers, educators, lawyers, and librarians. A variety of interest groups lobbied Congress to develop some specific guidance, particularly for educators, regarding fair use. Groups representing both intellectual property rights holders and those who would most likely take advantage of fair use wrote sets of "safe harbor" guidelines for print, music, and broadcasting. They are the "Agreement on Guidelines for Classroom Copying in Not-for-Profit Educational Institutions with Respect to Books and Periodicals" (Classroom Guidelines, 1976), "Guidelines for Educational Uses of Music" (1976), and "Guidelines for Off-Air Recording of Broadcast Programming for Educational Purposes" (1979).

These guidelines give specific minimum thresholds for fair use and are not law. They provide specifics such as amounts that can be copied (e.g., one chapter in a book, a complete poem under 250 words), types of copying, and operational definitions for many of the terms of fair use. They are intended as a definitive safety zone as "there may be instances in which copyright which does not fall within the guidelines … may nonetheless be permitted under the criteria of Fair Use" (Classroom Guidelines, 1976, p. 8).

In *Copyright Law on Campus*, Lindsey characterizes the Classroom Guidelines as "the most conservative and least contentious ground of fair use considerably biased in favor of commercial interests" (2003, p. 27). Although these guidelines are not law and represent a minimal threshold for fair use, it is common to see them in school policies as the upper limit of fair use (Talab, 1999, p. 30). Confusion about the fair use factors and the misuse of the safe harbor provision in educational policy can have a chilling effect on the legitimate invocation of fair use by teachers.

Guidelines for the fair use of multimedia were developed in 1996 by the Conference on Fair Use. They specify limits for the educational use of video, audio, and images without receiving permission from the rights holder (e.g., 3 minutes of a movie, 30 seconds of a song). These guidelines, though not law, are in numerous policies in school districts and colleges, despite the fact that they are opposed by organizations such as the Association of Research Libraries, the American Library Association, the National Association of School Administrators, the National Education Association, the U.S. Catholic Conference, and the National Association of Independent Schools (Association of Research Libraries, 1997). Indeed, in response to these guidelines, the Association of Research Libraries called on its members to "resist relying on any proposed code of conduct which may substantially or artificially constrain the full and appropriate application of fair use" (Association of Research Libraries, 1998, n.p.).

Digital Rights Management

Until recently, much of the decision-making powers in applying fair use have been in the hands of individuals. However, digital technologies that have enabled the reproduction of content are now able to substantially limit the use of this content. The printing press, photocopy machine, and VCR have worked with little distinction between authorized or unauthorized reproduction. A photocopy machine would not stop working for a particular magazine article without a secret password from the publisher. Although some anticopying technologies were on VHS tapes, these seem crude in comparison with the variety of restrictions now available on digital material with digital rights management (DRM) technologies. The initial outrage of the music industry about peer-to-peer networks such as the original Napster has been matched by the intricate technologies that are now embedded in online music, movies, books, and images.

Digital rights management is an umbrella term that covers the technologies used to restrict and control the use of digital content. For example, several years ago it was typical to download, share, save, and play an audio file in a way similar to using most other files on your computer. Today, DRM technologies embedded in the music file itself can control its use. These features can control the number of times you can play a song, the number of computers you can have it on, or the brands of portable players you can save it to. The types of restrictions are seemingly infinite. These DRM technologies are being applied to audio, video, books, and articles.

These DRM technologies pose a fundamental problem to English teachers. There is a basic conflict between these technologies and the fuzzy guidelines that educators rely on under fair use. A policy brief by Michael Godwin (2006) of the American Library Association states that the tensions between fair use and DRM are inevitable because "DRM tends to be precise and immutable, while our copyright law policy tends to be general and dynamic" (p. 2).

Copyleft

Although the full consequences of DRM policies on education will be an unfolding story of benefits and costs, it can be more useful to focus on initiatives that aim to allow for a more flexible use of other people's intellectual property. Such use is referred to as *copyleft* and related to the open source movement. One of the most noteworthy efforts is Creative Commons. The Creative Commons Web site (www.creativecommons.org) offers creators of intellectual property the ability to register their original works with a sliding scale of restrictions and freedoms. An author, photographer, or musician can license a work for noncommercial or nonderivative activities. For example, a photographer can allow others to use an image for nonderivative use in which the original image can be used, but not altered. Or, a musician can share a song with an attribution restriction; this allows people to download, share, and even profit from it, but gives credit to the original musician. (See Creative Commons licenses for more details, http://creativecommons.org/licenses/.)

Typically, Creative Commons licenses come with a symbol (Figure 1) and link, and their popularity is growing. Beginning in November of 2005, Google started to allow users to do an advanced search for material with Creative Commons usage rights.

Figure 1. Creative Commons logo

Creative Commons Attribution License 3.0

Flickr (www.flickr.com) and Openphoto (www.openphoto.net) are online photo-sharing services that let you search by Creative Commons licenses. The sites hold millions of images taken by people from around the world with numerous tags and categories as diverse as macro photography (extreme close-ups), historical sites, old typewriters, and the Middle East. When members upload images, they can select a Creative Commons license. This is an option on Flickr, but all the images on Openphoto have a Creative Commons license.

Many music sites also license with Creative Commons. Magnatune (www.magnatune.com), Opsound (www.opsound.org), GarageBand (www.garageband.com), and Dance-Industries (www.dance-industries.com) all have original music with Creative Commons licenses. GarageBand has a helpful search feature that allows you to search for original music that sounds like a particular band or song. The Freesound Project (http://freesound.iua.upf.edu) is an excellent source for sound effects (music is explicitly barred) with Creative Commons licenses. The ccMixter site (http://ccmixter.org) has Creative Commons music and audio samples (simple sound clips), and remixes using these sound clips. There is a growing Creative Commons movement in online video as well with sites such as Internet Archive (www. archive.org), Our Media (www.ourmedia.org), and Revver (www.revver.com), which allow downloading and varying methods of Creative Commons licensing.

Back to Ms. Mulvahill

Ms. Mulvahill explained the legal and ethical problems of using copyrighted music on the Web to her students. The most likely result would be a cease and desist order from the record company to the Internet service provider (ISP), in this case MySpace, and immediate removal of the offending material. This sounded "cool" to the students and some of them were willing to take that chance, but Ms. Mulvahill explained the ethical ramifications as well as the fact that they might be thrown out of MySpace.

She proposed using songs with Creative Commons licenses by Magnatune, ccMixter, and GarageBand. This explanation from Magnatune (2006) captures the expansive sharing allowed with these licenses:

> All our 128k mp3s are available under the "Attribution-NonCommercial-ShareAlike" license from Creative Commons to promote these goals. Specifically, this means:
>
> • You can listen to our Internet radio stations, download our free music, and share with anyone you like.

- *Derivative works (for example: remixes, cover songs, sampling) are explicitly allowed. Some of our artists publish the "source code" to their music so you can rework and improve it. This includes scores, lyrics, MIDI files, samples and track-by-track audio files. If you make a great new version of our music, we'd love to know so that we can promote it!*

- *Non-commercial use of our music and its "source code" is free. However, if you make money ("commercial use") with our music, you'll have to "share the wealth" and give us and our artists a share. (n.p.)*

Although a few students were familiar with these services, they did not realize the implications of the licensing agreements and options. The students substituted new songs for the commercial ones that they had originally used. The students were also surprised by the quality of the less restrictively licensed music and downloaded songs for their own listening. Next time Ms. Mulvahill does an assignment with media, she will have students initially use Creative Commons material and teach them the varieties of licensing.

Points to Ponder about Copyright

Keep the following information in mind when you encounter copyright issues in your classroom.

Students' work is copyright protected too. Work produced by students (and teachers) is as protected as the work of major recording artists and writers. No one can use your work—writing, music, or video—without your permission, except if they follow fair use guidelines.

Copyright law is meant to help the creator of the work as well as the public. Copyright limitations and fair use allowances aim to balance the creator's right to make money and society's right to improve itself with knowledge.

There are no clear-cut rules for fair use. You need to know the four factors and use your judgment. Don't be scared to use material in your classroom, and be wary of defined and prescriptive limits.

Materials with Creative Commons licenses are excellent resources. If you have aspirations for sharing your students' work on the Internet, use sources with Creative Commons licenses. You can cover a lot of current educational and ethical issues if you teach the students why these are acceptable.

Works Cited

Agreement on guidelines for classroom copying in not-for-profit educational institutions with respect to books and periodicals (Classroom Guidelines). (1976). H.R. Rep. No. 94–1476, pp. 65–74. As excerpted in United States Copyright Office/Library of Congress. (1998). *Reproduction of copyrighted works by educators and librarians* (Circular 21). Retrieved August 7, 2007, from www.loc.gov/copyright/circs/circ21.pdf

Association of Research Libraries. (1997). *Educational fair use guidelines for multimedia: A summary of concerns.* Retrieved January 25, 2006, from www.arl.org/info/frn/copy/mmedia.html

Association of Research Libraries. (1998). *Conference on fair use of copyrighted works concludes without consensus; educators, scholars, librarians to explore next steps.* Retrieved January 25, 2006, from www.arl.org/info/frn/copy/confustate.html

Fair Use, 17 U.S.C. § 107 (1976).

Godwin, M. (2006, January). *Digital rights management: A guide for librarians.* American Library Association. Retrieved August 7, 2007, from www.ala.org/ala/washoff/WOissues/copyrightb/digitalrights/DRMfinal.pdf

Guidelines for educational uses of music. (1976). H.R. Rep. No. 94–1476, pp. 65–74. As excerpted in United States Copyright Office/Library of Congress. (1998). (Circular 21). Retrieved August 7, 2007, from www.loc.gov/copyright/circs/circ21.pdf

Guidelines for off-air recording of broadcast programming for educational purposes. (1979). H.R. Rep. No. 97–495, pp. 8–9. As excerpted in United States Copyright Office/Library of Congress. (1998). *Reproduction of copyrighted works by educators and librarians* (Circular 21). Retrieved August 7, 2007, from www.loc.gov/copyright/circs/circ21.pdf

Lindsey, M. (2003). *Copyright law on campus.* Pullman, WA: Washington State University Press.

Magnatune. (2006). *What is "open music"?* Retrieved August 1, 2007, from www.magnatune.com/info/openmusic

McDonald, S. (2004, July 14). *Fair use and academic publishing.* Transcript from Colloquy Live, the Chronicle of Higher Education. Retrieved August 4, 2007, from http://chronicle.com/colloquylive/2004/07/copyright/

Stanford University. (2005). *Copyright and fair use.* Retrieved August 7, 2007, from http://fairuse.stanford.edu

Talab, R. S. (1999). *Commonsense copyright: A guide for educators and librarians* (2nd ed.). Jefferson, NC: McFarland & Co.

United States Copyright Office. (2000). *Copyright basics* (Circular 1). Retrieved August 7, 2007, from www.copyright.gov/circs/circ1.html

University of Texas. (2005). *Fair use of copyrighted materials.* Retrieved August 1, 2007, from www.utsystem.edu/OGC/intellectualProperty/copypol2.htm

CHAPTER **4**

Student Research in the Digital Age

THE WEB OFFERS TREMENDOUS opportunities for student research, yet it can also be a source of trouble and trepidation for teachers. Before we address the problems and opportunities that the Web offers for student research, we should candidly look at the state of student research before the Web. Despite the longings for easier days, there was never a "Golden Age of Student Research." Student research was not easy to teach for many of us before the Internet. In my case, teaching students research was isolated in a month-long unit. We would slog through a unit on "research" and then move on to other topics in the curriculum. I would try to coordinate the students' research topics—"What Is Hamlet's Problem?" or "The Life and Times of Fitzgerald"—with the books in the school library, books I brought in from home, and photocopies of articles that I had saved from college. There was a sense of a forced march, a march with limited rations and only a vague sense of mission.

I discovered that my experience was common as I commiserated with other teachers. Almost invariably we would shift most of the blame to the students, but in the back of my mind I knew I was missing something. Besides my own limited skills and experience, our school, like many, lacked the books or other resources to tackle a variety of research topics. There was a general sense that research skills in school had few immediate and transferable applications to students; student research was seen primarily as preparation for college. This was my experience as both a teacher and a student before the World Wide Web.

Of course, some extremely skilled teachers would have a research project with the resources on a particular subject stocked in the classroom or library. They knew how to teach students to approach the topic, what the books in the library had to offer, and what a good student paper would look like. Their research projects moved like clockwork. I'm sure that many have been able to apply their organizational skills to research in the age of the Internet. For most, however, the Web offers new challenges and possibilities.

Both the way we access information in our everyday lives and the landscape of resources for student research have fundamentally changed in the last 10 years. The emphasis on information literacy rather than literary research has created a sea change in teacher responsibilities. Information is coming from everywhere—encyclopedias, wikis, blogs, bogus Web sites, newspapers, crackpots, and experts in the field. Students are swimming in sources. The need to effectively evaluate and synthesize ideas and facts from many sources is a daily requirement that goes beyond a month-long unit.

There is no easy way to establish the credibility of a source. With multiple sources of data come varying levels of quality and credibility. Many people are using blogs as news sources, evidence of a growing consensus of their trustworthiness. This trend goes beyond the consumers of media and is becoming widespread among producers of news. I have repeatedly seen major news organizations use blogs as story sources, a development that challenges established standards of authority.

In the not so distant past we worried about the control of our information, and journalist A. J. Liebling's quip that "freedom of the press is limited to those who own one" was on classroom walls and office doors in schools and colleges in the United States for years. Today in the United States almost anyone can have the freedom of a virtual printing press—with a circulation of millions. Blogs and the Web have created a breed of citizen journalists and evenhandedly given soapboxes to the sublime and ridiculous. Although many individual Web sites are poor sources of information, some have earned readers' trust with expertise and credibility over the course of time and are establishing reputations that rival those of the mainstream media. You'll find similar circumstances regarding traditional sources: some people treat newspapers and magazines such as *The Washington Post*, *The New York Times*, *The Weekly Standard*, and *The Nation* as holy books, while others view them with utter skepticism because of biases, perceived or real. What guidance can we give students with these contradictions and changes? This problem grows exponentially when students have to synthesize multiple sources into a coherent and original research project.

Problems with Research Projects

I recently gave a workshop on student research to 14 teachers. A week before we began, I asked them to write down the biggest problems associated with student research projects. These ideas did not have to involve technology, yet Web issues are laced throughout their concerns. Here are the responses.

- Students just copy and paste from a Web site without citing the source.

- They are using the first few sources that pop up in the search without determining their validity.

- Students can buy or copy entire papers.

- They didn't have the patience to look up more than one source.

- They don't know what keywords to use for search engines.

- Writing with original thought is so daunting for students, but I believe we also need teachers who will accept original thought as the correct answer.

- I have found that the most difficult task of researching is determining what information is important. When my students were researching authors back in October, I noticed many of the students were overwhelmed by the wealth of information and forgot what facts they needed for the assignment.

- Reliability and accuracy are another big problem. It can take a lot of time to determine whether a site is reliable and factual.

- Students face the most basic of problems when it comes to using information from any source. They are easily confused with the topic of "copying." They don't understand the differences between copying, sharing, and using information in an appropriate manner.

- The difficulty students have when finding information is the difference between fact and opinion.

- Students don't have a plan for their research. If they don't know what they are looking for, how will they know if they find it?

- Being able to read and understand the information on the Internet can be a major problem for many. Because they have not developed note-taking skills, they tend to copy or print all the information they find.

- I have found that many times the information is above the student's reading comprehension level.

- My students have difficulty putting the research in their own words. Many times they want to just cut and paste information.

Common Misconceptions about Web Resources

To exacerbate these concerns, I have seen misinformation concerning the evaluation of Web resources, and these misconceptions get perpetuated. Here are some common misconceptions that I have repeatedly seen in Web site evaluation checklists and rubrics.

The domain name .org is better than .com. Either top-level domain name .org or .com can be purchased by anyone for any purpose. Students need to check the sources—read the About or Info sections of a Web site carefully. This can give clues to potential bias in legitimate Web sites. Also, use the Links To feature in the advanced searches of major search engines. This shows you who links to a site and provides context and commentary on its content and reputation.

An e-mail address is important to establish credibility on a Web site. Many junk mail bots get their spam lists from e-mail addresses on the Web. Many people are hesitant to put e-mail addresses on a Web page for this reason.

The date that the page was updated tells you how recent the information is. Many Web pages have server-side applications that automatically update the date on a Web page. This can be a misleading indicator of the page's age.

You can trust mainstream sources. While there are some sources that are considered authoritative for a particular field, mainstream sources should also be viewed with skepticism. Encourage the corroboration of facts as much as possible, unless you have a good reason to forego this step. This is an excellent habit to foster in students.

Popularity means credibility. This is the way most search engines and academic scholarship work—credibility by aggregation. A peer-reviewed journal article is considered more important the more it is cited, and a page with more links to it comes up higher in most Web searches, Google included. While there are obvious benefits to acknowledging ideas that have a broad acceptance, it is a trait that should be examined and discussed in the classroom.

Why Assign Research Projects?

Revitalizing student research cannot be done with quick fixes or simple checklists. It involves a fundamental reconsideration of why we give students research projects. Looking at the reasons can help teachers develop effective projects, lessons, and assessment techniques. Consider the following questions.

1. What types of research are educationally worthwhile?
    a. What makes research meaningful in a high school English class?
    b. What types of projects correlate with the way people need to research outside of school, in professional and everyday experiences?

2. How do you evaluate the credibility and importance of sources and facts?
    a. What makes a source credible?
    b. What material can students access on the Internet?
    c. What are the relationships and responsibilities among researcher, source, and audience?

3. How do students develop their ideas by incorporating multiple sources of information?
    a. What methods are useful to help students take ownership of ideas and facts?
    b. How can we capitalize on a student's prior knowledge and interest in a topic?

4. How can students clearly and compellingly present their ideas?
    a. What are the qualities of a good student research project?

      b. What are some alternatives to a research paper that correlate with activities in professional life and everyday experience?

  5. How do you teach students to adhere to ethical and legal standards when using other people's work and ideas?

      a. What are the reasons for a student to cite someone else's work?

      b. When is it unethical to use someone else's words or ideas?

A unifying idea that answers these questions is the cyclical process of student learning. The process is both internal and social; students internally revise their prior knowledge through social interactions with other people—interactions in forms as various as reading, having conversations, and watching YouTube videos. Synthesizing existing knowledge with correlating and contradictory information has been a model of learning from Plato to Piaget to proponents of new literacies.

The power of an audience, real or imagined, does a lot to guide student research. Identifying audiences and putting students in authentic or simulated roles (memoir writer, broadcaster, reviewer, activist, senator, journalist, movie director) that reflect actual activities outside of school motivates students and provides a support system of reasons and expectations for their work.

It is not only students who need a "why," but also teachers. Deeply reflecting on the "why" of conducting research on a particular topic can help teachers create meaningful projects. Teachers have to consider the reasons for these research projects beyond simple explanations such as their presence in the curriculum or that "students need to learn research." We not only need to give students reasons beyond compliance to an assignment and a grade, but we need to deeply reflect on the pedagogical goals of teaching research.

Five Steps for Research Projects

I have identified five steps for research projects—generated from my work and research with students and teachers. These five steps are interrelated. They are not linear steps, but can occur out of order or simultaneously. However, for designing and guiding student research, there is value at looking at them distinctly.

Step 1: Choose a Topic

The student chooses an initial topic or guiding idea such as a thesis. This guiding idea can change during the course of the research as the student collects information. To capitalize on a student's interest and sense of volition, give students choices and flexibility in the topic selection whenever possible. After choosing a topic, the student begins research based on the student's existing idea of the topography of the topic. Then, through readings and discussions with the teacher, the student refines this topography. He or she also begins to identify high-quality and credible sources.

Step 2: Collect Information

As the student is collecting information, he or she is analyzing it. The student begins to develop a hierarchy of information by asking: What is a major idea? What are supporting ideas? What facts correlate? Is there contradictory information? What information is not important? The student is also refining the idea of credibility and quality in regard to sources as well as modifying the initial idea and schema. Reading similar facts or ideas from multiple sources reinforces the importance of those facts and the credibility of a source. It is an internal process because it involves recognizing patterns and priorities. There is also a social component as the student becomes a participant in a community of people who care about this topic. For example, when students go to Web sites and blogs about U.S. history, they are participating in a community of historians, professional and amateur.

Step 3: Organize and Synthesize Information

The student organizes and synthesizes the information. How do the credible and important pieces fit together? What details are important for the work? The student is extending and refining the process that he or she started in Step 2. The student will probably need to go back and modify the topic or collect more information. Here, the external information is becoming internalized. The challenges to prior knowledge are both changing and reinforcing the student's mental schema on the topic.

Step 4: Articulate a Point of View

The student articulates a point of view. The student needs to explain the main ideas and supporting detail as well as accommodate ambiguous or contradictory information. Articulating ideas on paper, in video, or in audio creates a strong connection between the personal and the social. The student is committing to a point of view and attempting to anticipate the expectations, background knowledge, and interest of an audience. As the ideas begin to meet the light of day through language (words, films, audio clips), the student will often find the need to further refine his or her schema or collect more information; this process is further reinforced through the revision process. Articulating a point of view involves a consideration of media and message. The student has to consider the effect that words, images, sounds, voice, or slides have on others. That is why motivating students to write *without* an audience (intended or real) is a much more laborious task.

Step 5: Make a Deadline

The student needs to make a deadline. Deadlines are important because a teacher needs to assess students' understanding at a particular time. A teacher should look at assessment as a way to provide feedback to students so that they can improve their performance—not to audit performance.

The research process on a particular subject can be incessant, like the research of a hobbyist such as a coin collector who is fascinated with a certain mint or a professional such as a cardiologist who constantly searches for better ways to assess health. Finding new material, incorporating it into an existing mental schema, and articulating and rearticulating concepts and relationships pertaining to a particular subject is an important part of many people's personal and professional lives.

While continuously studying subjects is an important part of student research projects, a deadline means a finished product—an artifact that represents a student's work at a particular time and place in his or her development. Aside from the need to assess students, deadlines are extremely helpful to the learning process because they emphasize finality. Often students will spend disproportionate energies on tangential or supporting details. The finality of a deadline helps students prioritize.

Collecting, organizing, and integrating information, and then articulating a point of view within a specific time frame are fundamental and interrelated steps to research. With this framework you can thoughtfully design and guide students in meaningful and deep learning with the Internet.

Points to Ponder about Student Research

Keep the following information in mind when students are involved in research.

Plagiarism can be mitigated by an engaging, reflective, and candid approach to research.
Plagiarism is an ethical and academic problem that comes in many forms—from the outright purchasing of papers to the rephrasing of another person's ideas without attribution. When original and engaging assignments are used, plagiarism decreases significantly, and it is easier to catch. A chief enabler of plagiarism is using the same canned assignments from teacher editions (or the unwritten *English-Teacher-Thing-To-Do Handbook*)—essays like "Compare and Contrast Dimmesdale and Chillingworth in *The Scarlet Letter*" or "The Use of Light and Dark Imagery in *Romeo and Juliet*." Try to start with original or unique papers and projects, ones that capitalize on student interests and identities. This way students will be less inclined and less able to plagiarize. This can cut down on the most egregious forms of plagiarism—the wholesale use of a paper from the Internet or from another student.

Research is an activity that we all do, all the time, and will need to do more of in the future.
Unfortunately, many academic literary projects are distant cousins to the types of research done in everyday life. This is partly a necessity as the English class is the best place to introduce students to Keats, Chaucer, or Twain, and all teachers need to teach some topics that are not part of the workaday world. This being said, there is no excuse for cocooning the work of the English class away from the outside world, especially in regard to the way the Internet and research are used.

Honesty is part of good research writing. Letting a reader know where you got your information makes for a stronger paper. It's referred to as transparency, and teachers and students should value it when they read and write. Citing sources shows that you have read other work in the field, and it gives your facts credibility. It also insulates you from the full blame for factual mistakes if you can point to your exact source. Students should be taught when and how to cite facts and quote a variety of sources—including the work of other students. I would strongly recommend an overt classroom culture of transparency. Practicing good citation as a teacher is an excellent way to model and to get into a healthy mindset.

You can write an original work and use other people's ideas. Good research papers are like good songs that remix and sample other songs to create something new. Students seem to have an unrealistic sense of what it means to write an original work. Indeed, it is my belief that many students plagiarize because of an unhealthy reverence for other people's work, which appears to set an unreachable standard for their own writing on the same topic. Faced with a seemingly insurmountable task of writing comparably, they cheat.

Some facts need more citation than others. When do I need to cite a fact that everyone might know? For cases where a fact is common or popular knowledge—such as Thomas Jefferson was the third president of the United States—you usually do not need to cite a source. However, if you say that Jefferson was an atheist or had a social phobia, ideas that can be disputed or are not well known, you should have citations. This will boost your credibility on that point, provide the reader with a link to further reading, and generally strengthen the power of your writing.

In general, the more sources a fact, opinion, or idea has, the stronger your point is. Wikipedia, a blog, or an interview can be good starting points for research, but students should develop the skepticism to double-check their sources. A student can quote a blog (*The New York Times* does) if they simply want to illustrate a point of view. A student can begin their research at Wikipedia, if they want a current perspective. But we need to teach students that they need to corroborate their research points, especially ones that are controversial or crucial to their work.

Paraphrasing does not alleviate the need to cite a source. I have often seen teachers tell students to paraphrase an encyclopedia to avoid plagiarism. Rewording this information (even when a student uses the best thesaurus) and not citing the source is not ethical and is an academic disservice. It is an exercise in self deception that teaches poor scholarship and unethical behavior. Let them write parts verbatim but have them cite the source and then say something in their own words about the information.

The decision to paraphrase or to quote directly is usually one of style. A writer might paraphrase an idea or state a fact and use his or her own wording to keep the flow of the prose. However, if a writer wants to emphasize the uniqueness or originality of the idea or a writer likes the way an idea is expressed, he or she can use a direct quote.

This book contains several units that focus on research and offer many scaffolding techniques to help students become astute researchers. Unit 1: Podcourse uses the model and values of journalism to encourage students to critically find, evaluate, and integrate information. Unit 3: Blogging and Independent Reading Projects directs students to use research to inform their reading decisions. Unit 4: Wikis: Building a Bridge to the 18th Century is designed to have students research, cite, corroborate, and verify sources as well as credibly use and distinguish among primary, secondary, and tertiary sources. Unit 7: Audio Interviews for Perspective and Analysis provides scaffolding for deep reading, analysis, and research with a literary text. Unit 8: Persuasive Communication: Sending a Video to Your Representative guides students to carefully craft documented and persuasive videos with credible media, sources, and references. Unit 9: Technology and the Research Paper addresses reasons, trends, and technological tools and databases for literary research today. Unit 11: iBard: Mastering Soliloquies through Performance and Audio Editing focuses on the need for the clear and ethical citation of media sources. All the units are designed to help students become more savvy creators and consumers of information.

SECTION 2

Resource Units

UNIT **1**

Podcourse

STANDARDS

ISTE NETS for Students	1, 2, 3, 4, 5, 6
IRA/NCTE Standards	4, 5, 6, 7, 8, 9, 11, 12

KEYWORDS

audio technology, podcasting, journalism, student research

OBJECTIVES

Students will:

- Critically listen to audio essays created by teens outside and inside their classroom and provide comments.

- Write and record essays that effectively connect personal experience with social and political issues.

- Listen to and critically respond to a variety of news stories.

- Research news stories on school, local, regional, national, or international issues that balance perspectives and convey ideas in an effective and meaningful way.

UNIT DESCRIPTION

This activity gives a teacher the tools and methods to start a student-run radio show and post it to the Internet as a podcast. It can be used in a general literature, composition, or journalism course. The podcast would make an excellent supplement to a school or class newspaper. This activity can be done in a computer lab or in a one-computer classroom. In addition to computer access, this unit requires an Internet connection and a microphone. Software options are numerous, including the popular Apple product GarageBand. If you do not have any audio-editing software to begin with, I would recommend Audacity, free and easy-to-use audio-editing software that works across platforms and operating systems. (See appendix A for more information on using audio and for links to tutorials.) This unit presents options for organizing, broadcasting, and assessing this project. This activity in an excellent example of an authentic learning experience—it has a purpose and an audience and it connects students to the larger community and world.

To complete this unit, students produce two distinct types of projects: audio essays and news stories.

Audio essays. Although the topics can be diverse, the salient feature of a audio essay is that it connects students' experiences with some larger social or political issue. Students will first become critical listeners of audio essays and then produce them. It is a structured, academically rigorous, and personally rewarding experience for students.

News stories. This project is based on principles of journalism and research. The news story is distinct from the audio essay in that it attempts balance in presenting the facts and follows more formal journalistic standards.

I would strongly recommend extensions such as book and music reviews; sports segments; interviews with students, staff, and people from the community; audio plays; and audio tours. Once you do the two projects in this unit, it will be easier to develop and assess others.

To see a range of examples and projects that can be done with podcasts in the high school English course, go to Podcourse (http://podcourse.blogspot.com). This is the public site of an online high school English class that I taught called Podcasting and Creative Audio. The course focuses on innovative student-created podcasts as well as the accompanying legal and ethical issues. You can see descriptions and student examples of audio tours, media reviews, memoirs, audio plays, and other projects.

TECHNOLOGY

Internet

Podcasting

Audacity audio-editing software

RSS feeds

Blogging

MP3 files

SUPPLEMENTARY RESOURCES

For a list of Web resources that is frequently revised and expanded, go to http://del.icio.us/cs272/podcourse/.

For this unit, please also refer to chapter 3 (on copyright) and appendix A (on using audio).

Resources for Teachers

AudioFeeds.org: http://audiofeeds.org/tutorial.php
 A tutorial on making an RSS file from scratch. Relatively simple and for the
 do-it-yourself types.

Blogs, Wikis, Podcasts, and Other Powerful Web Tools for Classrooms (Richardson, 2006)
 An excellent description of new technologies and trends and their current applications.

FeedBurner: www.feedburner.com/fb/a/podcasts
  An automated way to turn a blog into a podcast using the enhanced RSS features provided by FeedBurner.

ListGarden: http://softwaregarden.com/products/listgarden/
  Free software that can generate an RSS feed for your audio files, turning them into a bona fide podcast.

Podcasting News: Making a Podcast with Blogger and FeedBurner:
www.podcastingnews.com/articles/Make_Podcast_Blogger.html
  A step-by-step guide to turning audio files into podcasts using Blogger and FeedBurner.

WNYC New York Public Radio: Soundcheck (NPR):
www.wnyc.org/shows/soundcheck/episodes/2006/05/16#segment60238
  It's a Pod World After All—a podcast on the state and variety of podcasting.

Resources for Teachers and Students

Apple iTunes: www.apple.com/itunes/
  The download site for the latest version of iTunes software. One of the most popular podcasting clients.

The Art of Foley: www.marblehead.net/foley/specifics.html
  Overview and examples of creating sound effects in the Foley artist tradition.

Art Mobs: http://mod.blogs.com/art_mobs/
  A podcasting initiative at Marymount College to create unofficial tours of art museums.

BBC Training and Development: Interviewing for Radio:
www.bbctraining.com/onlineCourse.asp?tID=2555&cat=3
  A free online training module from the BBC for conducting radio interviews.

Chris Shamburg Homepage: Audacity Tutorial: http://Web.njcu.edu/sites/faculty/cshamburg/
  This Web site offers a user-friendly tutorial for Audacity audio-editing software. It has all the audio files you need to learn the basics of audio editing, and takes 30–45 minutes to complete.

The Education Podcast Network: www.epnWeb.org
  A clearinghouse for educational podcasts. This is a great place to see and hear a variety of educational and classroom podcasts.

Library of Congress Learning Page: Using Oral History:
http://memory.loc.gov/learn/lessons/oralhist/ohguide.html
  An instructional unit and supporting material for doing oral histories.

Podcasting News: www.podcastingnews.com
  A source for updates and stories on podcasting.

Podcasting News topic: Podcast Software (Clients):
www.podcastingnews.com/topics/Podcast_Software.html
  A comprehensive list of podcasting clients.

Youth Radio (NPR): www.youthradio.org
  An initiative to encourage, develop, and disseminate audio essays from American teens.

Resources for Music and Sound Effects with Podcasting-Friendly Usage Rights

Creative Commons: www.creativecommons.org

Creative Commons Mixter: www.ccmixter.org

Dance-Industries: www.dance-industries.com

The FreeSound Project: http://freesound.iua.upf.edu

GarageBand: www.garageband.com

Magnatune: www.magnatune.com

Opsound: www.opsound.org

Audio Search Engines

FindSounds: www.findsounds.com

Podscope: www.podscope.com

Podcast Hosting Sites

Blip TV: www.blip.tv

DivShare: www.divshare.com

Ourmedia: www.ourmedia.com

Podcast News Sources

CNN Podcasting Archive: www.cnn.com/services/podcasting/archive.html#longform

Newsweek Podcasts: http://feeds.newsweek.com/podcasts/onair/

New York Times Podcasts: www.nytimes.com/ref/multimedia/podcasts.html

NPR Podcast Directory: www.npr.org/rss/podcast/podcast_directory.php

Podcasts from BBC News: http://news.bbc.co.uk/2/hi/programmes/4977678.stm

ACTIVITIES

Your first step is to set up your podcast. There are a variety of simple ways to do this.

This unit is organized as an eight-week project that would roughly coincide with a marking period. You can modify it to suit your needs such as extending it to a full school year or having weekly or monthly broadcasts.

A podcast is an audio file that comes to a listener. Will Richardson (2006) calls it "the creation and distribution of amateur radio, plain and simple" (p. 112). Creating the audio file is relatively easy—look at appendix A for a tutorial on Audacity audio-editing software or download Audacity (http://audacity.sourceforge.net) and begin experimenting yourself. If you know how to use a word processor and a tape recorder, you can learn Audacity easily. Just get an $8.00 microphone, and you can create and remix an audio file.

Once you create the MP3 audio file, you need to distribute it using an RSS feed. RSS is the technology that turns an MP3 file on a server into a podcast that people can subscribe to. The RSS feed is a file that updates a podcast client (a software or Web site such as iTunes that keeps track of and manages podcast subscriptions, also known as a podcatcher). You can create this file yourself or have it automatically generated by a Web application. The Resources for Teachers section provides links for a variety of methods to create the RSS feed file. Again, it's an easy technology. If you can fill out a form on the Web and follow simple directions, you can set one up in less than an hour. With your MP3 files and your RSS feed, you have a podcast.

Another important technology for this unit, though not for podcasting, is a Web-based commenting feature. Students will need to comment on their classmates' work after they listen to them.

While there are a variety of technologies that can offer the RSS and commenting features on your school's server, I would recommend using existing commercial services at little or no charge. DivShare (www.divshare.com), Ourmedia (www.ourmedia.com), and Blip TV (www.blip.tv) are three podcast hosting sites. They will host your MP3 files as well as generate your RSS feed. Or, you can use a blogging software. For a step-by-step explanation on how to turn your audio files into podcasts with Blogger (www.blogger.com), go to Making a Podcast with Blogger and FeedBurner (www.podcastingnews.com/articles/Make_Podcast_Blogger.html). I would recommend creating a single site that you would be the sole moderator for. This would index the students' work and generate the RSS.

WEEKS 1–2

Students listen and respond to audio essays created by a variety of teens.

Begin this unit with a description of podcasting and the features your students will include in their podcast—the audio essays and the news stories. For the first two weeks, introduce students to the audio essay. If you choose to use Audacity and students are not familiar with it, have them do the tutorial listed in Supplementary Resources. Through this exercise, they can get a functional understanding of the software. If you are using different software, such as GarageBand, and students are not familiar with it, set aside a day or two to introduce the software. The tutorial can be modified for that software. You need to give your students the skills they require to record, insert, and manipulate audio files.

The first project is the audio essay, in which students create recordings that connect their personal experiences to social and political events. This project makes excellent use of existing nonprint texts—projects from NPR's Youth Radio (www.youthradio.org)—and embeds developmental principles of writing and learning. The audio essay is cognitively demanding, addresses higher-order thinking skills, and is intrinsically motivating to students. Getting students to craft audio essays that connect their lives and experiences to the larger world and then share their projects can be an ongoing process.

Before your students begin creating audio essays, they should listen to and discuss them in a structured and intelligent way. In class and for homework, have students listen to the five audio essays listed in Handout 1.1 and answer and discuss the questions in Handout 1.2. All of the essays come with text transcripts. They are available as an MP3 file and through a podcasting client and can be downloaded, burned to a CD, or saved on an iPod or other digital audio player. The titles and descriptions of the segments are from NPR. After students have listened to these essays and answered the discussion questions, ask them to write, record, and revise their own audio essays. You can spend a day on each essay and then a day or two comparing them all.

WEEKS 3–4

Students create their own audio essays for podcasting and intelligently respond to their classmates' work.

Following the directions on Handout 1.3, students will write and record two audio essays. I would strongly recommend a peer-editing approach at the writing or recording stages; you can use or modify the peer-editing process described in unit 5. Because the labor and time is spent on writing, revising, and conferencing about the essay, the students can work in a classroom with a limited number of computers or even in a one-computer classroom. You can organize the writing and speaking parts to optimize the students' time based on the resources in your class and at your school. Ideally, your class will run like a functioning lab, with students alternating between writing, recording, and conferencing.

After the students have written and recorded two essays, it is time to "go public." I understand the hesitancy of exposing students' work on the Internet, so this can be done with a spectrum of levels for access—within a classroom, a school, or the world. You can also refer to Handout 1.7, especially if you are putting students' work on the Web. This contract represents a conservative stand on using podcasting in your class and can be modified for your class and students. You should also review Jo McLeay's classroom blogging guidelines in unit 3. She has some excellent guidelines for making students' work public.

Building on the skills that your students developed when they responded to the initial set of audio essays as well as when they created their own essays, they will comment on their peers' work (Handout 1.4). These questions encourage students to go beyond quick or facile responses. This is when they will use the commenting feature of your site. I recommend having students listen to at least eight student essays and comment on five of them. You can assign the essays, let the students pick, or mix assigned essays and student choice. You do want to ensure that each student gets feedback on his or her essay. Having students comment on each other's work democratizes the ideas of print and nonprint texts and gives the students an audience for production and feedback.

You can vary the procedures and contract, but a conservative and simple approach would be to have a single podcast show (from a single blog with a single RSS feed) that the teacher controls. The teacher can upload the students' MP3 files to a school server and link to them in the blog. The students would be responsible for writing brief descriptions of the audio essays and subsequent projects.

WEEKS 5–6

Students become critical listeners of the news.

We will now add news stories to your students' repertoire in your class podcast. Students will again begin by becoming critical listeners; this time it will be as listeners of news features. Download a variety of podcasts from the following sources. You can use a podcasting client or download the files directly from these sites.

- CNN Podcast Archive
  www.cnn.com/services/podcasting/archive.html#longform

- Newsweek Podcasts
  http://feeds.newsweek.com/podcasts/onair/

- New York Times Podcasts
  www.nytimes.com/ref/multimedia/podcasts.html

- NPR Podcasts
  www.npr.org/rss/podcast/podcast_directory.php

- Podcasts from the BBC
  http://news.bbc.co.uk/2/hi/programmes/4977678.stm

After your students have listened to a selection of news stories (in class and/or for homework), have them answer and discuss the questions in Handout 1.5. After preparing students to be intelligent consumers of information, you will have them create news features. They should use Handout 1.6. You can modify it to suit your students and classrooms. You might also want to call attention to techniques that break conventional rules of reporting, such as a buried lead (circuitously stating the main idea of the story). You will be focusing on the fundamentals of journalism as the students create audio news stories on local, regional, national, or international events. This work will emphasize the five Ws (who, what, when, where, and why) and the one H (how). It will also emphasize the importance of balance and source citation in news stories. This project is best done in small groups of two to four students.

Assessment

These two rubrics are for the projects described in this unit. You should distribute these to the students. Optimally, you should distribute and review a rubric after you have introduced the project and all of its components, but before students begin substantive work on it.

Rubric for Audio Essay

	Approaches	Meets	Exceeds	Relevant ISTE NETS•S	Relevant IRA/NCTE Standards
Content of recording	Little or no connection between personal experiences and social issues	Connection between personal experiences and social issues	Strong connection between personal experiences and social issues	1, 2, 3, 4, 5, 6	4, 5, 7, 11, 12
Articulation *(please note that this is to be based on the individual student's potential. Students with speech difficulties should not be penalized.)*	Little concern for clarity, pace, or spoken techniques (inflection, tone, pauses, etc.)	General concern for clarity, pace, and spoken techniques (inflection, tone, pauses, etc.)	Great concern for clarity, pace, and spoken techniques (inflection, tone, pauses, etc.)	1, 2, 6	4
Organization of recording	Ideas are not organized or presented in an effective way	Ideas are generally organized and presented in an effective way	Ideas are consistently organized and presented in an effective way	1, 2, 3	
Language in recording	Inappropriate use or lack of stylistic techniques (e.g., figurative language, transitions, varied sentence types)	Adequate use of stylistic techniques (e.g., figurative language, transitions, varied sentence types)	Effective use of stylistic techniques (e.g. figurative language, transitions, varied sentence types)	1, 2	4, 5, 6, 9

Rubric for News Story

	Approaches	Meets	Exceeds	Relevant ISTE NETS•S	Relevant IRA/NCTE Standards
Five Ws and the H addressed	Few or some addressed or addressed inadequately with supporting detail	All or most addressed adequately with supporting detail	All or most addressed substantially with supporting detail	1, 2, 3, 4, 5, 6	8
Sources cited *(including explanations of anonymous sources, if applicable)*	None or few sources are cited appropriately	Most sources are cited appropriately	All sources are cited appropriately	3, 5	7
Source quality	Sources lack diversity and credibility	Sources demonstrate a general diversity and credibility	Sources demonstrate a consistent diversity and credibility	3, 5	7, 8
Perspectives	Single or limited perspectives	Attempt to give balanced perspectives	Effectively and substantively illustrates multiple perspectives	3, 5	7, 8
Length	Length of segment inappropriate for style and content	Length of segment generally appropriate for style and content	Length of segment effective for style and content	2	4, 5

Work Cited

Richardson, W. (2006). *Blogs, wikis, podcasts, and other powerful Web tools for classrooms.* Thousand Oaks, CA: Corwin Press.

Teaching with Fanfiction

STANDARDS

ISTE NETS for Students	1, 2, 5, 6
IRA/NCTE Standards	1, 2, 3, 4, 5, 6, 11, 12

KEYWORDS

creative writing, fanfiction, peer editing, online collaboration

OBJECTIVES

These objectives might need to be slightly modified based on the choices you make in designing the unit. Students will:

- Produce creative writing projects in various fanfiction genres based on source material.

- Read a variety of source material and transformative and derivative works from published authors and peers, both online and in print.

- Provide meaningful feedback and commentary to peers regarding creative works.

- Demonstrate an understanding of the artistic, historical, creative, and legal relationship between source material and transformative and derivative works.

Fanfiction refers to the cultural phenomenon in which fans write and share fictional works based on the stories that capture their interests. The most popular sources for fanfiction are Harry Potter and other fantasy and science fiction movies, books, and television shows. However, works such as *Pride and Prejudice*, the Bible, and *1984* have been popular sources of fanfiction as well, all inspiring fans to write sequels, prequels, missing scenes, and retellings of the original stories from the perspectives of diverse characters.

Literary history is full of such textual filching—authors, playwrights, and poets creating original literature based on the characters and settings of others. This type of literary appropriation is so pervasive that it can be seen across authors and periods from antiquity to today. The *Aeneid* is Virgil's sequel to Homer's *Iliad*, a story of the survivors of the decimated Troy. Boccaccio, Chaucer, and Shakespeare all wrote stories about Troilus and Cressida, star-crossed lovers of the Trojan War. Although Troilus and Cressida never appear in Homer's works, they have been put in Troy with missing scenes and alternative points of view on the war. Milton's *Paradise Lost* supplies missing scenes from the Bible and Twain's *A Connecticut Yankee in King Arthur's Court* mixes the universes of Arthurian legend and 19th-century industrialism.

More recent and self-consciously derivative examples are Stoppard's *Rosencrantz and Guildenstern Are Dead* and Gardner's *Grendel*. In fact, the 2006 Pulitzer Prize for fiction went to Geraldine Brooks for *March*, the story of the missing father from Alcott's *Little Women*.

The modern phenomenon of fanfiction predates the Internet, but has grown and thrived online. Fans of particular books, movies, TV shows, and video games go online to write original fiction based on their favorite stories and then read, revise, collaborate, and comment on them with fans who share their passion. Online blogging communities such as LiveJournal and sites such as FanFiction.Net have become more than repositories of fanfiction; they are communities of readers and writers who provide commentary, share enthusiasm, offer proofreading, and collaborate on creative pieces. The fanfiction community has developed a vocabulary with terms such as *fanon, Mary Sue,* and *spackle*—terms that facilitate communication and reinforce the sense of fandom (see Fanfic Vocabulary).

Fanfic Vocabulary

Fanon. Information or characterization that has never been confirmed in canon (the original source material) but is accepted as such by fans.

Mary Sue. Any original or deeply altered character who represents a slice of his or her creator's own ego.

Spackle. This is a story that tries to "fill in the holes" in canon, supplying missing scenes or motivation.

All definitions from Fanfiction Glossary (www.subreality.com/glossary/terms.htm).

Throughout literary history and fanfiction one can see creative and original literary works springing from a captivation with the source material and the compulsion to expand on it. Almost any teacher who has seen students reading, writing, and commenting on fanfiction with engagement and care must have an inclination of its potential for teaching and learning, especially creative writing. The idea of derivative and transformative works is not new in literature or in teaching; this unit proposes a model to capitalize on the creative and successful aspects of fanfiction.

The overarching educational approach to this unit is the theory that learning involves a deepening participation in a community of practice. Jean Lave and Etienne Wenger (1991) are credited with articulating this theory of learning, and it has to varying degrees informed theory and policy in education for the last decade. The premise is that an individual begins on the periphery of a community and moves toward the center of that community as he or she learns the language, skills, knowledge, and mindsets of the community members. Learning is seen as a social process rather than the acquisition of discrete skills.

The community in which you want to engage your students is the community of skilled readers and writers. Whether or not they are involved in fanfiction, many students come to your classes with a set of literary skills. This skill set could include reading, viewing, discussing, and writing material of interest to them. This interest might focus on comic books and graphic novels, romance stories, science fiction novels, young adult literature, or even complex video games such as *Myst*. Although their scope of interest might be limited, kids understand narrative, characterization, and plot in their stories because these stories resonate with them. Through activities related to fanfiction and derivative literature, you can deepen their participation as writers and readers. This is done by creating work based on their interests and letting them take ownership of existing literature.

SUPPLEMENTARY RESOURCES

For a list of Web resources that is frequently revised and expanded, go to http://del.icio.us/cs272/fanfiction.

For Teachers

Academic Treatments of Fanfiction

Convergence Culture (Jenkins, 2006)
> This book addresses larger trends of participatory culture and contains an especially compelling chapter about fanfiction, "Why Heather Can Write."

The Democratic Genre: Fan Fiction in a Literary Context (Pugh, 2006)

Fan Fiction and Fan Communities in the Age of the Internet (Hellekson & Busse, 2006)

Textual Poachers (Jenkins, 1991)

Other Fanfiction Resources

The Fanfiction Glossary: www.subreality.com/glossary.htm
> Detailed, comprehensive, and balanced dictionary of fanfiction.

The Mary Sue Project: www.hbook.com/publications/magazine/articles/nov06_almagor.asp
> Article in *Horn Book Magazine* about an innovative way to use fanfiction techniques in language arts—innovative and inspiring.

Rewriting the Rules of Fiction: http://online.wsj.com/public/article/ SB115836001321164886-GZsZGW_ngbeAjqwMADJDX2w0frg_20070916.html
> Article in *The Wall Street Journal* chronicling the popularity of fanfiction.

When Lit Hits the Fans: http://observer.guardian.co.uk/review/story/0,,1933977,00.html
> Article in *The Guardian* about the growing popularity of fanfiction.

For Teachers and Students

Derivative and Transformative Stories

Ahab's Wife (Naslund, 1999)
Story of the wife of Ahab from Moby Dick.

Angel and Apostle (Noyes, 2005)
Young adult literature that focuses on Pearl's life from child to young woman after the time of *The Scarlet Letter.*

Foe: A Novel (Coetzee, 1987)
Robinson Crusoe from Friday's perspective.

Gertrude and Claudius (Updike, 2000)
A prequel to *Hamlet* focusing on the story of Hamlet's mother and uncle.

Grendel (Gardner, 1971)
The dragon's perspective of Beowulf.

A House-Boat on the Styx (Bangs, 1895)
The underworld peopled by literary and historic characters.

The Last Temptation of Christ (Kazantzaki, 1951)
The story with Jesus with a Jesus different than the Bible's version.

Mary Reilly (Martin, 1990)
The maid's version of *Dr. Jekyll and Mr. Hyde.*

The Mists of Avalon (Zimmer Bradley, 1982)
The King Arthur legend told from the women's perspectives.

Rosencrantz and Guildenstern Are Dead (Stoppard, 1967)
An absurdist version of *Hamlet* from two existential protagonists.

Snowball's Chance (Reed, 2002)
A sequel to *Animal Farm* in which the collective goes capitalist.

The True Story of the 3 Little Pigs (Scieszka, 1989)
The story of the pigs from the wolf's perspective. Some students might be familiar with this book from their own childhood. Even if they are not, it is a clear way to introduce the concept of derivative and transformative literature and multiple perspectives. This is a good example (though not quite appropriate reading for high school students) for a discussion on the topic.

"Ulysses" (Tennyson, 1842)
Poem exploring the aging Odysseus's desire for travel and contempt for his homeland years after returning from his odyssey. Available at www.gober.net/victorian/ulysses.html from Susan B. Horton.

Wicked: The Life and Times of the Wicked Witch of the West (Maguire, 1996)
The Wicked Witch's story from the *Wizard of Oz.*

Wide Sargasso Sea (Rhys, 1966)
The life of the woman in the attic in *Jane Eyre*—what brought her there and how she went mad.

The Wind Done Gone (Randall, 2001)
   Gone with the Wind from the slaves' perspective.

Sources of Fanfiction on the Web

Fanficrants: http://fanficrants.livejournal.com
   I would especially like to recommend and thank the members of the LiveJournal community Fanficrants for their feedback and support for this unit.

FanFiction.Net: www.fanfiction.net
   Collective of fanfiction in numerous categories

Jane Austen Fanfiction Sites: www.austen-beginners.com/fanfiction.shtml
   Clearinghouse of Jane Austin fanfiction.

Shoebox Project: http://community.livejournal.com/shoebox_project/
   Popular fanfiction on Harry Potter's parents before Harry.

Blogging Software

Classblogmeister: www.classblogmeister.com

Gaggle: www.gaggle.net

Learnerblogs: http://learnerblogs.org

21 Publish: www.21publish.com

TECHNOLOGY

   Internet

   Word processing

   Wikis

   Blogs

ACTIVITIES

There are many options to consider when implementing this unit that would affect your timetable. So instead of including a suggested schedule like in the other units, I have focused on the areas that need to be taken into account when developing and teaching a writing unit based on fanfiction. Here are the four distinct yet interrelated areas that you need to consider:

1. Reviewing the fanfiction genres

2. Choosing the audience and materials (classroom audience or public audience; teacher-selected materials or student-selected materials)

3. Encouraging high-quality feedback

4. Broadening the skills and interests of your students

REVIEWING THE FANFICTION GENRES

When developing writing projects on fanfiction, you should be familiar with some of the popular genres of fanfiction. What type of "fiction" will your students be writing? The choices of genre will also depend on your decisions about audience and, especially, materials. However, it is difficult to begin working with fanfiction without a basic understanding of its genres. Here genre does not refer to a specific subject (such as mystery or romance) or specific format (such as drama, poetry, or prose), but rather genre refers to the concept of the original fiction. Based on the genres and the source material, you can design appropriate schedules for drafts, timetables for peer editing, and required minimum lengths for writing products.

The following items are based on genre definitions from fanfiction (The Fanfiction Glossary, 2005) and have been delineated to facilitate teaching. There is some debate on several of these definitions, so you might want to acknowledge this fuzziness to any purists in your class. I have included literary examples in parentheses.

- **Missing scenes.** These scenes are not in the original story, but would be consistent with the original story. Typically, the missing scene would respect the facts and characters of the author, referred to as the canon in both fanfiction and conventional literary terms (*Rosencrantz and Guildenstern Are Dead*, Stoppard).

- **Alternate perspective.** The story is told from a different perspective. This is an important leitmotif in postmodern literature and characterizes recent trends in literary criticism. This can be an opinion about a character, an event, or the entire story. It strongly connects to unit 7 (which includes character interviews) and unit 9 (*Ahab's Wife*, Naslund).

- **Alternate universe.** A major character or event in a story is changed, by the instructor or the student, and a "What if …" scenario ensues (Gnostic Gospels).

- **Alternate realities.** Characters from one story or world enter another story or world (*Inferno*, Dante).

- **Sequel.** A story after the timeline of the original material (*Angel and Apostle*, Noyes).

- **Prequel.** A story before the timeline of the original material (*Wide Sargasso Sea*, Rhys; The Shoebox Project, Jones & Rave).

- **Self insert.** The story is rewritten to include an avatar (a representation of the author). See "The Mary Sue Project" (Almagor, 2006) for an excellent detailed unit on this (*A Connecticut Yankee in King Arthur's Court*, Twain).

These genres can be combined as well. For example, you could have a prequel from an alternate perspective (*Gertrude and Claudius, Angel and Apostle*). Furthermore, a common subgenre of all fanfiction genres is a drabble, a work of a specific and short length, traditionally 100 words, usually done as an exercise or challenge.

CHOOSING THE AUDIENCE AND MATERIALS

There are two related decisions to make when designing a unit based on fanfiction. You need to decide who your students will be writing for and what they will be reading. The first decision is to choose your audience. Will you work within your classroom or post student work publicly on the Internet? The second decision relates to the material you will use. Will you use teacher-selected material or student-selected material? Each decision comes with a spectrum of possibilities. For example, students can share work beyond their classroom but within their school's intranet, though not with the general public on the Internet. Also, students can use a prescribed story, a list of acceptable stories, or choose the material themselves and use it based on the teacher's approval.

The following activities are generally associated with each of the four major directions based on these choices: a classroom audience, an audience on the Internet, *teacher-selected material*, and *student-selected material*. The terms student-selected material and teacher-selected material are open to some interpretation. The general distinction is the amount of control that the teacher will have on the students' choices.

You can use a single model, a combination, or all four, based on the scope and flexibility of your curriculum and your teaching style. If you use student-selected material, keep an open mind during the selection process. You or your students might want to use literature such as the Harry Potter books, movies such as *Star Wars*, or TV shows such as *Gilmore Girls*. There are benefits and values to emphasizing the "fan" in fanfiction. Students will likely be more motivated and you can still teach writing skills and expand their interests. The following chart depicts the four combinations that can characterize your work based on your decisions of audience and materials.

	Teacher-Selected Materials	Student-Selected Materials
Classroom Audience	Classroom Audience Teacher-Selected Materials	Classroom Audience Student-Selected Materials
Public Audience	Public Audience Teacher-Selected Materials	Public Audience Student-Selected Materials

The sections that follow discuss teaching ideas related to the different choices of audience and material.

Classroom Audience

Fanfiction has been fueled by the Web, but this unit can be successful in a classroom with or without networking technology. However, even if you decide not to post student work publicly on the Web, you can use a secure blogging or wiki system to allow students to remotely read and comment on the work of their peers. Crucial to this assignment is the ability of students to read and respond to each other's work; it can be done orally in class with little or no technology or it can be done with a closed and secure blogging system.

A blogging system allows student to edit and add installments as well as comment on each other's work. A variety of free blogging software allows for private and secure access within a class or school, such as the following:

- Classblogmeister: www.classblogmeister.com
- Gaggle: www.gaggle.net
- Learnerblogs: http://learnerblogs.org
- 21 Publish: www.21publish.com

Lelac Almagor, an English teacher at the National Cathedral School for Girls in Washington, D.C., uses an activity based on fanfiction when she has her students write themselves in as characters in novels that they are reading (Almagor, 2006). It is a fascinating project with a brilliant technique to introduce the students to literary analysis (giving students a 10-minute, high-energy collaborative task and then asking them to analyze their communication). Almagor finds that students "quickly discover that fitting a new character into the story means dismantling the original prose to see how it works." Almagor's "Mary Sue Project" is an excellent example of the teaching possibilities of fanfiction techniques. This project incorporates a consideration of racial identity, literary analysis, and reader identity in an engaging way. Her article in *Horn Book Online* (www.hbook.com/publications/magazine/articles/nov06_almagor.asp) should be required reading for any English teacher who wants to engage students in reading and writing.

Public Audience

The Web offers the widest audience for readers of fanfiction based on traditional or popular literature. Many fanfiction sites are out there, but I would recommend posting on FanFiction. Net, a large and popular outlet for fanfiction. Writing for a large audience is an extremely motivating factor, particularly when the audience is familiar with the topic and shares an interest in the subject matter. FanFiction.Net has a variety of existing categories for literature—including Homer, Jane Austin, 1984, and Fitzgerald—and users are allowed to create categories. Other sites specialize in certain authors, books, and TV shows.

You can also set up a community on FanFiction.Net, a C2. As the moderator of a C2 you can collect fiction from a variety of authors in one site. You can also add staff members to collect material. Your students could staff the C2 with the responsibility of submitting original work and other material related to your topics or genres.

The benefits of using a public site come with risks. Although FanFiction.Net is dedicated to supporting the creation and sharing of fanfiction, students can access adult material there. Participation in FanFiction.Net requires registration, and the site has strict policies against harassment and procedures for labeling mature content. Nevertheless, students are often two clicks away from mature material. If you believe that this service is within the community standards of your school and curriculum, it can be a powerful tool for student writers. Otherwise, you can select high-quality and appropriate work from the site and share it with your students yourself.

Another option is a Web-based blogging system or wiki. You could also have students begin their own fanfiction site, where you or they control the content.

Regardless of how you use the Internet, soliciting feedback from a variety of readers is an important characteristic. Students are writing for the larger community of readers, writers, and fans. Admittedly, this feedback can be brief and superficial, but examining ways to improve feedback is an important and teachable activity and a component of this unit.

When placing student work publicly on the Web, you should consider the current state of copyright law and the connection to fanfiction. Many authors and media outlets believe that fanfiction boosts their work and overtly or tacitly support its creation (Jurgensen, 2006). Meg Cabot, author of the Princess Diaries series, is flattered by the amount of fanfiction her stories generate and admits to once being a writer of fanfiction herself (Jurgensen, 2006), while Anne Rice actively discourages her fans from writing it (Rice, 2004).

Legally, there is a distinction between derivative and transformative works: a transformative work has distinct elements of originality. Individual pieces of fanfiction can be considered either violations of copyright or unique pieces of intellectual property. For a complete overview, see the Chilling Effects Clearinghouse FAQ on fanfiction (www.chillingeffects.org/fanfic/faq.cgi).

If you want to decrease or eliminate the potential for copyright infringement, you can focus on works that have a strong fanfiction base or that are out of copyright. Please note that copyright infringement only becomes a potential problem when posting on the Internet. Use of fanfiction in class seems like an obvious example of fair use. Please read chapter 3 for more information on fair use.

Teacher-Selected Materials

Stories that the teacher selects which are part of the traditional high school curriculum can be fertile sources for projects based on fanfiction. You can give the students choices on the type of fanfiction genres you want them to do, such as a prequel, sequel, or self insert. For example, if you are working on a short story such as Poe's "The Cask of Amontillado," genres such as prequels, alternate perspectives, or missing scenes would seem to work the best. A focus on Fortunato's side of the story would be an interesting activity.

Here are some sample ideas that use popular books from the high school curriculum.

- ***The Adventures of Huckleberry Finn.*** Write a sequel with Huck involved in the Civil War.

- ***Dracula.*** Create an internal monologue from Dracula.

- ***Pride and Prejudice.*** Develop a story in which a modern American goes back in time and becomes Elizabeth's confidante and advisor.

- **"The Raven."** Write a prequel, in poetry or prose, from the point of view of Lenore.

Here are some existing categories on FanFiction.Net that correlate with many high school curriculums. You can get high-quality samples from these locations or have students post their work.

- Charles Dickens: www.fanfiction.net/l/1352/3/0/1/1/0/0/0/0/0/1/

- The Crucible: www.fanfiction.net/l/1710/3/0/1/1/0/0/0/0/0/1/

- Fairy Tales: www.fanfiction.net/l/892/3/0/1/1/0/0/0/0/0/1/

- Fitzgerald (mostly Gatsby): www.fanfiction.net/l/1481/3/0/1/1/0/0/0/0/0/1/

- Greek Mythology: www.fanfiction.net/l/1366/3/0/1/1/0/0/0/0/0/1/

- Jane Austen: www.fanfiction.net/l/1237/3/0/1/1/0/0/0/0/0/1/

- Little Women: www.fanfiction.net/l/2663/3/0/1/1/0/0/0/0/0/1/

- The Odyssey: www.fanfiction.net/l/1713/3/0/1/1/0/0/0/0/0/1/

- To Kill a Mockingbird: www.fanfiction.net/l/757/3/0/1/1/0/0/0/0/0/1/

- Wuthering Heights: www.fanfiction.net/l/2298/3/0/1/1/0/0/0/0/0/1/

Student-Selected Materials

Letting students pick their source material can be an extremely powerful way to connect to their interests and then broaden and deepen their skills as readers and writers. I'd like to offer a few general instructions. First, all selections should be approved by the teacher. Second, you should capitalize on the students' desire to share their interests with others. Students broaden their participation as readers and writers not only when they read works recommended by others, but also when they share and explain their interests with others. Students should provide an overview of their source material (Handout 2.1). This is an opportunity for critical reflection and a way to develop the analytical skills of explaining a fictional world to others.

ENCOURAGING HIGH-QUALITY FEEDBACK

A significant part of this project is encouraging students to provide high-quality feedback on the work of other students. Several units describe scaffolding techniques for student feedback (notably unit 4 and unit 5). Commenting on fanfiction follows similar lines. Have students include the following elements in their comments. It might seem forced and difficult at times, but it will train them to be thoughtful communicators.

- Begin with a positive comment (unless the work is obviously careless or awful). Teaching students to be collegial members of a community is an important lesson.

- Comment on the points of interest or originality of the work. This is the purpose of writing fanfiction—to maintain an audience's interest by using a new approach to familiar material.

- Comment on the consistency with source material, the canon (not adhering to the canon is not a value judgment per se, but a characteristic of the work). The connection to or deviation from the source material is a fundamental element of fanfiction and literary works based on source material.

- Add suggestions for improvement—this can be in style, plot, mechanics, or other literary elements. The key is to offer suggestions to make it a more engaging and interesting piece.

- Comment on the general state of the spelling, grammar, and expression, and possibly add specific suggestions.

BROADENING THE SKILLS AND INTERESTS OF YOUR STUDENTS

The overarching goal of this project is to deepen and broaden your students' skills as readers and writers. Figure 2 gives a sketch of some of the possible characteristics and activities that a student will move through, beginning on the outside and moving toward the center. It is the job of the teacher to facilitate this movement and prevent students from getting stuck on the periphery. Being mindful of this process can help a teacher capitalize on opportunities for broadening their interest as well as assist the teacher to focus on the guiding principle of the unit. Remember, you are beginning with the students' creativity and interests and then broadening the literary interests and deepening their writing and reading skills.

Figure 2. Fanfiction skills in a community of practice

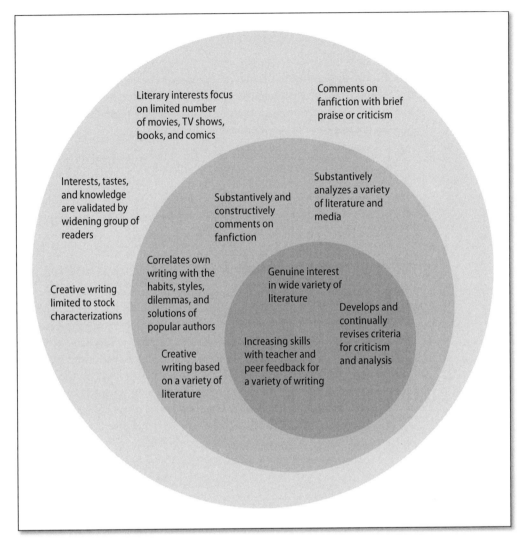

Literary interests focus on limited number of movies, TV shows, books, and comics

Comments on fanfiction with brief praise or criticism

Interests, tastes, and knowledge are validated by widening group of readers

Substantively analyzes a variety of literature and media

Substantively and constructively comments on fanfiction

Correlates own writing with the habits, styles, dilemmas, and solutions of popular authors

Genuine interest in wide variety of literature

Develops and continually revises criteria for criticism and analysis

Creative writing limited to stock characterizations

Creative writing based on a variety of literature

Increasing skills with teacher and peer feedback for a variety of writing

Assessment

Below is the rubric for the fanfiction project. You should distribute the rubric early in the unit, so students know the values and expectations of the project. You should then revisit and revise a rubric with each student in a conference as you review his or her work together.

Rubric for Fanfiction Project

	Approaches	Meets	Exceeds	Relevant ISTE NETS·S	Relevant IRA/NCTE Standards
Writing	Works do not follow the characteristics of the given genres and have minimal or limited creative elements	Works generally follow the characteristics of the given genres, contain original elements, and are written in a clear and interesting way	Works follow the characteristics of the given genres, are quite original, substantively engage the reader, and are written in clear and engaging language	1, 2, 6	3, 4, 5, 6, 12
Providing feedback	Student does not follow the criteria for feedback and provides few or superficial comments	Student generally follows the criteria for feedback and provides several helpful comments	Student follows the criteria for feedback and provides many substantive comments	2, 5, 6	3, 4, 5, 6, 11
Reading	Student does little or no reading	Student reads a variety of works in a few genres from a few sources	Student reads a variety of works in multiple genres and from multiple sources—from both the literary canon and peer fanfiction, online and in print	6	1, 2, 11
Understanding of the relationship between source material and original works *(as demonstrated in the writing, commenting, reading, and class discussions)*	Student is unable to articulate an understanding of the relationship between source material and original works	Student articulates an understanding of the relationship between source material and original works—in either their own writing and reading or in the writing of others	Student articulates an understanding of the relationship between source material and original works—in their own writing and reading and in the writing of others	1	1, 2, 4, 11, 12

Works Cited

Almagor, L. (2006, November). The Mary Sue project. *Horn Book Online*. Retrieved August 7, 2007, from www.hbook.com/publications/magazine/articles/nov06_almagor.asp

The Fanfiction Glossary. (2005). Retrieved August 7, 2007, from www.subreality.com/glossary.htm

Jurgensen, J. (2006, September 16). Rewriting the rules of fiction. *The Wall Street Journal Online*. Retrieved August 7, 2007, from http://online.wsj.com/public/article/ SB115836001321164886-GZsZGW_ngbeAjqwMADJDX2w0frg_20070916.html

Lave, J., & Wenger, E. (1991). *Situated learning: Legitimate peripheral participation*. Cambridge, UK: University of Cambridge Press.

Rice, A. (2004). Writing archive. Retrieved August 7, 2007, from www.annerice.com/fa_writing_archive.htm

UNIT **3**

Blogging and Independent Reading Projects

by Jo McLeay

STANDARDS

ISTE NETS for Students   1, 2, 4, 6

IRA/NCTE Standards   1, 2, 3, 4, 7, 8, 11, 12

KEYWORDS

blogs, RSS feeds, independent reading, summer reading, novels

OBJECTIVES

Students will:

- Collect appropriate resources from the Internet to create reading lists.

- Read from a broad range of texts.

- Interpret and discuss texts with other students using blogging software.

- Build an understanding of their text, themselves, and others to produce a creative response to their novel.

- Apply their understanding of the novel to generate a problem or question for exploration by other students.

- Deliver an oral presentation to the class on their novel.

UNIT DESCRIPTION

Independent reading projects are a powerful tool to connect students to literature based on their interests. However, structuring, monitoring, and assessing students' success in independent reading projects is a challenge for teachers—whether it's during the school year or for a summer reading assignment. This unit outlines a model for designing an independent reading project using technology in innovative ways. Through the use of blogs, RSS feeds, online book clubs, and social bookmarking, teachers can create successful experiences for students to discover, read, and discuss great literature.

For students who are readers, this sort of assignment is no problem. There is often a problem with reluctant readers. These are students who haven't yet been introduced to the "break-through book" or the "home run book," as Stephen Krashen (2004) calls it—sometimes just one good experience can hook someone into reading for life. This unit incorporates the social aspects of reading, student-made "top 10" lists, social software, and technology that appeals to high school students.

This unit uses blogging to get students discussing books with each other even if they are on their summer break. Students may have been introduced to blogging in other classes, but if this is their first experience, Handout 3.3 talks about some things they should know (blogging rules and etiquette). A teacher who blogs with her students once asked other teachers why they blogged in their classrooms. A summary of the answers follows: Blogging with students is worthwhile to engage students in a purposeful practice of writing that can support deep learning. Students get to practice writing and expressing their opinion through a diverse array of writing experiences. It's a way we can let our students know that their writing matters. Blogging also allows students to learn about connecting their ideas with others, revising their thinking, and considering the ideas of others in a public space. It allows for the quiet students to express their thoughts. It creates the feel of a learning community in a place away from the traditional classroom—a place that is open 24/7. It is a communications method that students must master to be effective contributors to society in their future. Most of all, students become engaged.

Blogging becomes even more powerful with the addition of RSS. What is RSS? This is a way of subscribing to Web pages so that it is easy to see when they have been updated. To subscribe it is necessary to have a free account with bloglines.com or some other aggregator of feeds (subscriptions). It is a very easy technology to use and makes blogging in a community of inquiry much easier. It would also be appropriate for you to subscribe to your students' blogs to see when it may be worth having a look and possibly leaving an encouraging comment.

In the course of this unit, students create several entries as well as comment on several blogs of their classmates; develop one response to their novel from the independent novel assignment and present it to the class; write a brief review of their novel that includes a star rating; and generate a problem or question about their novel for the following year cohort.

TECHNOLOGY

Computer availability

Internet access for each student

Blogging and RSS software

SUPPLEMENTARY RESOURCES

Resources for Teachers

Amazon's Top Listmania Lists: www.amazon.com/gp/richpub/listmania/toplists/
Listmania lists are a great way to share knowledge with others.

Authentic Persuasive Writing to Promote Summer Reading:
www.readwritethink.org/lessons/lesson_view.asp?id=312
 A Read/Write/Think lesson plan with great resources.

Going with the flow: How to Engage Boys and Girls in Their Literacy Learning
(Smith & Wilhelm, 2006)

Librarything: www.librarything.com
 The Librarything site helps you create a library-quality catalogue of your books.
 You can catalogue all of them or just what you're reading now.

Librivox: http://librivox.org
 Librivox provides free audiobooks from the public domain. Students may find books
 they want to read here in audio form.

The Power of Reading: Insights from the Research (Krashen, 2004)

Ray Saitz Independent Novel Assignments: http://home.cogeco.ca/~rayser3/indst92.txt;
http://home.cogeco.ca/~rayser3/windst2.txt
 Ray Saitz has developed an excellent collection of activities on his Web site.

Social Bookmarking Sites

Social bookmarking is a way of saving Internet resources to a Web page that allows them to
be accessed from any Internet-connected computer. This system is "social" in that lists can
be tagged and shared, thus making it an easy way to find suitable resources. Two of the most
popular sites for literature are:

 Ma.gnolia.com: http://ma.gnolia.com
 del.icio.us: http://del.icio.us

Blogging: Resources from English Teachers Who Blog with Their Classes

Blog2Learn: http://adavis.pbwiki.com/Guidelines%20and%20Responsibilities

The Cool Cat Teacher Blog:
http://coolcatteacher.blogspot.com/2006/08/how-to-comment-like-king-or-queen.html

Langwitches: www.langwitches.org/blog/?cat=2

The Open Classroom: http://theopenclassroom.blogspot.com

Random Thoughts:
http://namckeand.blogspot.com/2006/03/and-yet-another-favor-to-ask.html

Class Blogs

My Year 8 English Experience: http://casper.learnerblogs.org/2006/
05/17/book-girl-underground-morris-gleitzman-and-refugees/

PC Writes: http://mccb.edublogs.org

How to Comment on Blogs

EduBlog Insights:
http://anne2.teachesme.com/2006/02/22/thinking-about-the-teaching-of-writing/

Resources for Teachers and Students

Reading Lists

Ashland Public Schools: http://www.ashlandhs.org/ahs/pdfs/AHSSummerRead07.pdf

Books for Girls: http://amlib.eddept.wa.edu.au/Webquery.dll?v20=MarcList&v24=509178&v40=4422&v46=4426

Fresno County Public Library: www.fresnolibrary.org/teen/bn/authors.html

Houston Area Independent Schools Library Network (HAISLN) Recommended Reading Lists: www.haisln.org/ReadingLists.htm

YALit: www.yalit.com

Young Adult Library Services Association (YALSA): Literature and Language Arts: www.ala.org/ala/yalsa/booklistsawards/outstandingbooks/litlanguage.htm

Young Adult Library Services Association (YALSA): Quick Picks for Reluctant Young Adult Readers: www.ala.org/ala/yalsa/booklistsawards/quickpicks/quickpicksreluctant.htm

Reading Ideas

Use the following resources to get ideas for books you or your students may like based on what has been enjoyed in the past.

Literature-Map: www.literature-map.com
    Enter a favourite author and the site will generate a map of new authors that you may like.

What Should I Read Next?: www.whatshouldireadnext.com
    Enter a book you like and the site will analyse the database of real readers' favourite books (more than 20,000 and growing) to suggest what you could read next.

Blogging Sites

Bloglines: http://bloglines.com

Learnerblogs: www.learnerblogs.org

ACTIVITIES

Although this unit is organized as a summer reading program while the students are on vacation, it can work equally well as a class project or simultaneously with other teaching units. This unit has six focus areas designed to get students reading and generate thoughtful discussions. They are:

1. A wide reading focus and the development and evaluation of lists

2. A blogging focus and the formation of online book clubs

3. An RSS focus to keep in touch

4. An independent novel assignment focus with an emphasis on reader response

5. A presentation focus to share with the class

6. A written focus for the next cohort of students

DAYS 1–2

Wide Reading Focus

Questionnaire and teacher discussion. It is important to prepare the students in their book selection. Taking time to do this also emphasizes the importance of the project itself. Independent reading projects can be presented and perceived as curricular add-ons instead of substantive work. During these initial classes, ask the students to brainstorm and list 5–10 books that they have enjoyed, either in school or on their own. Then give students a questionnaire to complete (see Handout 3.1). This questionnaire gets the students thinking about their reading experiences. Reviewing the results and, if there is time, calling up students individually for a one-to-one discussion on reading, can help the teacher know the students better and think of books that may help particular students. This activity, while the class is working quietly on something else, develops an atmosphere of discussion and helps students see that their opinion is important. It can also be a very enjoyable activity for the teacher.

List activity. Following on from the questionnaire and discussion, have students produce a list of their personal "top 10" books from Internet research and lists supplied by the teacher (see Handout 3.2). Where do the lists come from? The teacher can collate a class list from recommendations on the student questionnaires. There are also various school reading lists in Resources for Teachers and Students. Literature-Map (www.literature-map.com) is free software that enables a search of a database starting from a student's favourite author. From this the student can find other books that he or she may like. For example, if you put in Ann Brashares, you find that other readers of this author are reading Megan McCafferty, Louise Rennison, Sarah Dessen, Jonah Black, Meg Cabot, Jenny Carroll, and Marya Hornbacher. Students can also find lists on Amazon.com through Listmania and recommendations from the Amazon community. Amazon.com also offers lists based on customer purchases, with a category titled "Customers Who Bought This Item Also Bought." Using these tools we may find that students interested in Anthony Horowitz may also like Eoin Colfer and Christopher Paolini.

Another idea to generate lists is to ask teachers and librarians at the school to recommend one or two books that they think may be suitable and to publish this list and the teachers' names together with a sentence or two describing it. This has a twofold benefit: it models that reading, while not often done at work, is something that we all are involved in, and it provides a wider range of books by using as resources educators who are not necessarily English teachers. In future years the lists can also come from the previous year's student recommendations.

Social bookmarking. Students can also search for items of interest to help them find books through social bookmarking sites such as http://del.icio.us and http://ma.gnolia.com. These sites also produce an RSS feed so they can be subscribed to through Bloglines.

Students look at some of the lists to come up with a brief reflection on what kinds of books are listed, and what kinds of books they would like to see on a list based on their research. When they bring their finished list to class, go around the room and ask each student to share one title from his or her list. This will validate the choices from each student. Then begin again; however, after the first student mentions another book, have the next student describe the book on his or her list that comes closest to this book based on the genre or features. There will be some close comparisons and some distant connections, and this is a good way to explore both the variety and connections in the student reading choices. Have students then choose a book or books to read over the summer break. All selections should be subject to the teacher's approval. Students should be allowed to change books if they are not happy with their choice. The student's choice should be paramount for engagement.

(Some of this section is based on NCTE's ReadWriteThink lesson plan on Authentic Persuasive Writing to Promote Summer Reading.)

DAYS 3–5

Blogging and RSS Focus

Set up each student with a blog from Learnerblogs (http://learnerblogs.org). Staying safe online is something we need to teach our students. Issues of privacy and security are not immediately obvious to students, and what we see as common sense needs to be taught to students who have not been taught this before. If they are familiar with blogging, a reminder may suffice, but this cannot be assumed. Students should not reveal their last names (or the last names of classmates) or the name of the school (or any personal information, such as birth dates, IM screen names, e-mail addresses, home addresses, or phone numbers) on their blogs or in comments, and they should not link to their school blog from a private blog (if they have one).

Before students begin to write in their blogs they need to be taught the use of appropriate netiquette, and it may be timely to have the students come up with some rules for blogging (see Handout 3.3 for a sample sheet). Show the students some class blogs (see http://mccb. edublogs.org and http://casper.learnerblogs.org/2006/05/17/book-girl-underground-morris-gleitzman-and-refugees/) and explain how to comment (see http://anne2.teachesme.com/2006/02/22/thinking-about-the-teaching-of-writing/). Students are required to write at least one post a week and to comment on two of their classmates' blogs while the summer reading project is on. There may seem like a lot of off-task commenting and blogging going on, but this is good. In between blogging, the students are expected to focus on their reading, but they associate it more with fun than with work. Blogging is also social, and research shows that students learn in social situations from one another. The foundation of Lev Vygotsky's (1962) influential theory of human development inextricably integrates social interaction and learning. We can see that learners reach a stage where social interaction must take place for additional progress to occur. Blogging very practically fulfills this need in students. Students who have chosen the same books can form online book clubs where they can share insights and questions with each other.

The next session may be a good one to have the student sign up for a free Bloglines account at www.bloglines.com and set up their RSS feeds. This allows the students to subscribe to their classmates' blogs so that they can immediately see when anyone has updated their blogs and go to the blog, read, and comment. Students can also subscribe to other blogs of interest and news updates on issues of concern.

DAY 6

Independent Novel Assignment Focus

This is when the independent novel assignment is introduced (see Handouts 3.4 and 3.5). This assignment is not based on comprehension questions or essays, but rather on a student-created artefact to show at school during an exhibition or oral presentation (see Handout 3.6). In this assignment student choice is important, as it is when selecting novels to read. The assignments are a mix of creative and applied writing and art activities. The finished product or digital images of it can be uploaded to the student's blog and reflected on there.

(Some of this section is based on ideas from Outta Ray's Head Web site, http://home.cogeco.ca/~rayser3/windst2.txt.)

ON RETURN TO SCHOOL

Oral Presentation and Written Focus

When students return to school, they are expected to do a three-minute oral presentation about the book they read, focusing on the appealing aspects of the novel and presenting the information in such a way as to be useful for students who may want to choose that novel in the future. You may want to organise an exhibition of the artefacts if appropriate. Students may need a digital projector to show the class their blog on a large screen. Students will be expected to hand up or have on their blog a brief review (about 50–80 words) of their novel that discusses the target audience, how enjoyable it was to read, what made it enjoyable (or not), and a star rating (to include in the list activity for following years).

Have students think about a question or problem that they feel is worthy of further thought by future readers of the novel (to include in the independent novel assignment for subsequent years). This information can be collated by the teacher for the next cohort of students.

Assessment

Use the following rubrics to assess the independent novel assignment and oral presentation. Distribute these and review them with the class after you have introduced the projects, but before students begin substantive work on them.

Rubric for Independent Novel Assignment

	Unsatisfactory	Satisfactory	Exceptional	Relevant ISTE NETS•S	Relevant IRA/NCTE Standards
Response to literature	Simple and rudimentary response. Unreflective in choice and execution of activity	Has made connections between characters and student's own life	Sophisticated, developed, and subtle understanding of the novel shown; draws on literary or cultural connections	1, 2, 4, 6	1, 2, 4, 11, 12
Evidence of thought	Little or no evidence of reflection on the themes or characters	Some evidence of reflection on the themes or characters. Has reflected on the significance of the themes	Shows a good understanding of self and student's own reading process, has reflected on symbols and settings in the novel as well as characters and themes	1, 2, 4, 6	3, 4
Creativity	Little or no creativity or original thought	Some creativity and originality is demonstrated in the choices made and the execution of the project	Highly creative and original in all aspects of the project	1, 6	3
Organisation	Not well thought out. Random decisions made about organisation	Well organised, in chronological order or order of importance	The organisation is shown to be an integral part of the presentation of the project; is logical and well thought out	1, 2, 4	4
Requirements, including Top 10 list	Incomplete	Complete		1, 2, 4, 6	1, 2, 7, 8, 11, 12

Rubric for Oral Presentation

	Unsatisfactory	Satisfactory	Exceptional	Related IRA/NCTE Standards
Awareness of the purpose and the audience *(the purpose is to persuade others of the appealing aspects of the novel; the audience is students who may want to read the book)*	Shows little awareness of the purpose or the audience. May tell too much of the plot	Shows awareness of the purpose and the audience	Highly informative and persuasive talk that shows excellent awareness of the purpose and the audience	2, 3, 4, 12
Vocal techniques	Pace too fast or too slow; voice is too loud or too soft; little or no eye contact	Pace is generally good; voice projection is well understood; eye contact is generally effective	Highly competent in vocal techniques of pace and delivery as well as engagement with the audience	4, 12
Use of palm cards	Palm cards not used or inappropriate in size; student is too dependent on them	Palm cards used competently, for occasional reference only; student is not overly dependent on them	Palm cards used very competently and unobtrusively	4, 12
Organisation	Little evidence of thought given to organisation	Talk is organised effectively with some use of signposting	Talk is effectively organised and signposted	1, 2, 3, 4, 12
Requirements, including Top 10 list	Less than two minutes	Two to three minutes	Three minutes	4, 12
Requirements including six blog entries and review	Incomplete	Complete		

Works Cited

Krashen, S. D. (2004). *The power of reading: Insights from the research.* Portsmouth, NH: Heineman.

Vygotsky, L. (1962). *Thought and language.* Cambridge, MA: MIT Press.

UNIT **4**

Wikis
Building a Bridge to the 18th Century

Figure 3. Piecing together Johnson

STANDARDS

ISTE NETS for Students	1, 2, 3, 4, 5, 6
IRA/NCTE Standards	1, 3, 5, 6, 7, 8, 11

KEYWORDS

wiki, 18th century, British literature, student research, peer editing

OBJECTIVES

Students will:

• Use technology to collaboratively create a database and a relational schema of knowledge.

• Research and verify information from a variety of sources (primary, secondary, and tertiary; print and electronic).

• Connect literature and history to contemporary issues.

UNIT DESCRIPTION

The 18th century is one of the most exciting and relevant time periods in Western history. However, it often suffers in the literature class because its breadth and depth are challenging, and because its position between the more popular topics of Shakespeare and the Romantic poets often leaves it overlooked. This unit helps teachers convey and connect the exciting literature, history, science, and philosophy of the period through the creation of a class wiki. In a structured and paced approach, students take ownership of knowledge and knowledge creation. They cite sources, check facts, and take responsibility for individual and collaborative research. This unit is inspired by Neil Postman's book *Building a Bridge to the 18th Century*, but it can be used for almost any period of literature, and would be particularly useful in studies of the Romantic or Victorian eras. Some of the best aspects of modernity—rationalism, humanism, civil rights, scientific methods—were developed, formalized, or popularized in the 18th century. Please remember that these concepts were not the sole purview of English-speaking people. This unit is limited to the events and people in the English-speaking world, but you can expand it to a multidisciplinary unit.

This unit connects the broad content of 18th-century literature with an appropriate method, a research wiki that the students create, revise, and verify. A wiki is a collaborative Web site. Its usefulness is facilitated by Web-based editing tools that allow changes from a Web browser—no downloads or special software required. The other useful aspects of a wiki are the tracking features. Most wikis allow log ins and attribute work to a user as well as allow a user to revert to a previous version of a page. Many offer comments sections so participants can have discussions on the content of a particular page.

The 18th century was eventful and can be a challenge to tackle in one unit. I would suggest using a timeline that starts with the Restoration (1660) and ends with the publication of Mary Wollstonecraft's *A Vindication of the Rights of Woman* (1792). This can be tweaked for your tastes, curriculum, time, or texts.

TECHNOLOGY

Wikis

Computers with Internet access

SUPPLEMENTARY RESOURCES

For lists of Web resources that are frequently revised and expanded, go to http://del.icio.us/cs272/wiki and http://del.icio.us/cs272/18thcentury/.

Resources for Teachers

Building a Bridge to the 18th Century (Postman, 1999)
> This book is the inspiration for this unit and its title. This unit can be seen as a clarification of or rejoinder to the Postman book, which addresses the stifling effects of technology on human development.

Discussing Neil Postman's *Building a Bridge to the 18th Century*:
www.futureofthebook.org/blog/archives/2005/09/podcast_discussing_neil_postma.html
> A podcast discussion of the book with multiple and divergent perspectives.

Educators Experiment with Student-Written Wikis:
www.edweek.org/ew/articles/2006/04/05/30wiki.h25.html
> An article in *Education Week* with examples and applications of wikis in schools.

Search vs. Research: www.marcprensky.com/writing/Prensky-Search_vs_Research-01.pdf
> This article offers a persuasive and cogent argument for the uses of Wikipedia and the distinction between searching on the Internet and using the Internet for research.

Wide Open Spaces: Wikis, Ready or Not:
www.educause.edu/pub/er/erm04/erm0452.asp?bhcp=1
> This Educause Review article gives a insightful overview of the uses and potential of wikis in education.

Writing Space: Computers, Hypertext, and the Remediation of Print (Bolter, 2001)
> A thought-provoking book on the implications of hypertext on the way we read, learn, and think.

Resources for Teachers and Students

Eighteenth-Century England: www.umich.edu/~ece/
  A selective and useful site of 18th-century resources created by literature students at the University of Michigan.

Eighteenth-Century E-Texts: http://andromeda.rutgers.edu/~jlynch/18th/etext.html
  Comprehensive list of online texts.

Eighteenth-Century Resources—Literature: http://andromeda.rutgers.edu/~jlynch/18th/lit.html
  A clearinghouse for 18th-century resources.

High School Online Collaborative Writing: http://schools.wikia.com/wiki/Main_Page
  A wiki project for student writing involving more than 20 New York City high schools.

Restoration & 18th Century: http://vos.ucsb.edu/browse.asp?id=2738
  A selective and useful site for 18th-century resources.

Wiki-Building Web Sites

PBwiki: www.pbwiki.com

Seedwiki: www.seedwiki.com

Wikispaces: www.wikispaces.com

ACTIVITIES

DAYS 1–3

Students are given terms and guidelines for creating their initial wiki entries.

Divide the class into four groups and give each group a list of terms to create their 18th-century entries (Handout 4.1). Each group must have a student take responsibility for one entry. The teacher can modify the lists depending on the number of students.

Each initial entry must include the following:

Text of the entry. Text amounting to 100–200 words (not including quotations or the reference list).

References in the text. References in the text (citations or quotations) from print or the Internet of at least:

- Two tertiary sources and one primary source, or

- One secondary source and one primary source

Tertiary citations must be corroborated by another tertiary, secondary, or primary reference (see Handout 4.2 for details).

Reference list. References must be separated by source type (primary, secondary, tertiary) and follow a standard format. This can be MLA format, a school format, or a format designed for your class or the wiki.

Figure 4 is an example of an entry for Alexander Pope. It contains all of the material required of an initial entry. Putting this information into a wiki page is as simple as using a word processing program. The figure 4 inset, a page from Pbwiki, illustrates what the information would look like on a wiki page.

Within the entry framework, students can cite literature as well as online encyclopedias. They can use various sources to corroborate information or to point out contradictions. The key is to cite sources and integrate them in the entry. Students can get primary, secondary, and tertiary sources from print or the Internet. They should cite the material and link when possible.

After they have researched and created their initial 18th-century entry, they will create their initial modern connection entry. The exciting part of this project is helping students see the connections between the 18th century and today. All of the initial modern connection entries must be related to today's world, and students should create these entries with the same criteria used for the 18th-century entries.

Figure 4. Example
of wiki entry for
Alexander Pope

Alexander Pope

Alexander Pope (May 21, 1688 to May 30, 1744) (Wikipedia, Britannica). Pope is an Eighteenth Century English poet who is most popularly known for his satirical poems and translations of Homer's Iliad and Odyssey (Wikipedia, Britannica). His most famous works are

- *An Essay on Criticism* (1711),
- *The Rape of the Lock* (1712. 1714)
- A translation of Homer's *Iliad* (1720)
- A translation of Homer's *Odyssey* (1726)
- *The Dunciad* (1728, First Version)
- *An Essay on Man* (1733–34)

His satire was especially sharp when he aimed it at his literary enemies, as he did in many of his works. For example,

> While pensive poets painful vigils keep,
> Sleepless themselves to give their readers sleep. (*The Dunciad*)

Pope is still quoted often even today. Here are some of his most famous lines.

> Hope springs eternal in the human breast:
> Man never Is, but always To be blest. (*An Essay on Man*)

> To err is human, to forgive, divine (*An Essay on Criticism*)

> A little learning is a dangerous thing;
> Drink deep, or taste not the Pierian spring. (*An Essay on Criticism*)

Tertiary Sources

"Alexander Pope." Encyclopedia Britannica. 2006. Britannica Concise Encyclopedia. 19 Sep 2006
http://concise.britannica.com/ebc/article-9375645/Alexander-Pope

"Alexander Pope." Wikipedia, The Free Encyclopedia. 17 Sep 2006, 17:28 UTC. Wikimedia Foundation, Inc. 19 Sep 2006
http://en.wikipedia.org/w/index.php?title=Alexander_Pope&oldid=76253642

Primary Sources

Pope, Alexander. *The Dunciad*. Poets' Graves. 19 September 2006
www.poetsgraves.co.uk/Classic%20Poems/Pope/the_dunciad_book_the_first.htm

—. *An Essay on Criticism*. Eserver Poetry Collection. 19 September 2006
http://poetry.eserver.org/essay-on-criticism.html

—. *An Essay on Man*. Eserver Poetry Collection. 19 September 2006
http://poetry.eserver.org/essay-on-criticism.html

(Continued)

Figure 4. *(Continued)*
Example of wiki entry
for Alexander Pope

Wiki Links

- Dunciad
- Satire
- Heroic Couplets
- An Essay on Man

Modern Connections

- Satire and the *Stephen Colbert Show*

Page from PBwiki.

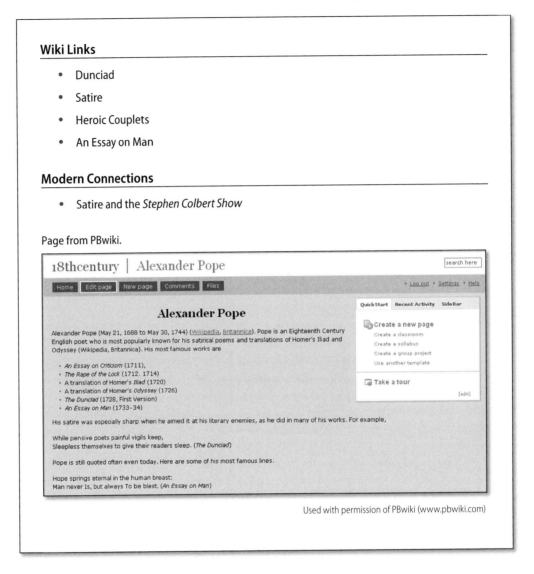

Used with permission of PBwiki (www.pbwiki.com)

For example, an entry about Johnson's *Dictionary* might connect to an entry about Wikipedia; an entry about *The Rights of Man* might connect to an entry about the current debate on security and civil liberties; and an entry on Thomas Hobbes might connect to examples of civil conflicts from around the world. This is an excellent opportunity to individualize instruction in mini-conferences with the teacher. The modern connection entry will be subject to the same process of revisions and comments as the 18th-century entry.

After students have created their initial entries, they will begin to explore the collaborative and networked powers of the wiki and hypertext. At the bottom of each entry, students must link two terms from their group and two terms from another group. The collaborative process of linking exposes the connections, interdisciplinary nature, and relevance of history. You can have the students link only the 18th-century entries or both the 18th-century and modern entries. This depends on your time, teaching priorities, and students. These links must connect to entries that are relevant to their work. They must also edit the entries that they linked to so that they link back to their entries. This is the first time they will be editing another student's work. It is a small modification, but a significant step in exploring the collaborative possibilities of a wiki.

DAYS 4–7

Students revise and comment on other students' entries.

During the next few days, the students increase their scope of responsibility and collaboration in creating knowledge. This is done through a scaffolded approach that gives the students directions that broaden and guide their work to improve in the knowledge creation. First, each student must take responsibility for the four entries that they linked to and correct, add, or modify the entries. There is a hierarchy of changes, and students have to address each of them. Students must:

- Research and correct any factual errors.

- Add any important elements that are missing.

- Delete any details that are unnecessary.

They must do this and not exceed the 200-word limit. This teaches students an economy of writing and encourages them to critically examine the facts and text of the author. They are now as responsible as the original author.

They must also comment on four entries in the entire wiki that they have not linked to. This forces them to broaden their reading and participate in a larger community. For this activity, have students use the wiki commenting feature to ask metacognitive questions about the process and entries. The following chart offers suggestions for comments.

Type of Comment	Sample Start of Comment
Other Contemporary Issues	This entry is related to another issue in today's world …
Other 18th-Century Issues	This entry should also be linked to …
Question on Inclusion	I still don't understand the importance of this entry because …
Comment on Significance	This is an especially important entry because …
Further Question	I have a further question on the subject that may or may not be important …

Although these types of overarching issues are not the sole purpose of commenting, it is important that students learn that commenting is an important process and plays a significant role in discourse. Too often, commenting by students on the Web is facile and brief. Students need practice in making substantive use of feedback tools on the Web.

As groups work more independently, you should distribute Handout 4.3 to the students so they can check their responsibilities and monitor their progress.

Assessment

Your assessment of this project will be based on a written report submitted by the students (see Handout 4.3) and your evaluation of their work on the wiki. The report is a road map for you to track and assess their work on this project. A rubric has also been provided to help you evaluate student work. Optimally, you should distribute the rubric and review it with students after you have introduced the project, but before students begin substantive work on it.

Rubric for Wikis

	Approaches	Meets	Exceeds	Relevant ISTE NETS•S	Relevant IRA/ NCTE Standards
Creates initial entry	Inadequately follows guidelines for text and references	Generally follows guidelines for text and references	Exactly follows guidelines for text and references	2, 3, 4, 5, 6	1, 3, 5, 6, 7, 8
Creates modern connection entry	Inadequately connects to 18th-century entry	Generally connects to 18th-century entry	Effectively and convincingly connects to 18th-century entry	1, 2, 3, 4, 5, 6	1, 3, 5, 6, 7, 8
Links to four related entries	Does not link to four related entries	Links to and links back from four related entries	Links to and links back from four entries that are highly related to original entry	2, 3, 4, 6	1, 3, 8, 11
Edits four entries	Inadequately follows guidelines for edits	Generally follows guidelines for edits	Exactly follows guidelines for edits	2, 3, 4, 6	1, 3, 5, 6, 8, 11
Comments on four entries	Inadequately follows guidelines for commenting	Generally follows guidelines for commenting	Exactly follows guidelines for commenting	2, 3, 4, 5, 6	1, 3, 5, 6, 8, 11
Produces final report with clear expression and full citations	Report is not clear and/or does not cite relevant pages	Report is clear and cites all relevant pages with minor deviation	Report is clear and cites all relevant pages	1, 2, 3, 4, 5, 6	1, 3, 5, 6, 7, 8, 11

UNIT 5

Memoirs and
Online Peer Editing

Figure 5. The Writer.
(Image by Clive Power, used with permission of Clive Power.)

STANDARDS

ISTE NETS for Students	1, 2, 4, 5, 6
IRA/NCTE Standards	1, 2, 3, 4, 5, 6, 8, 11, 12

KEYWORDS

reluctant readers, ESL, ninth grade, online collaborations, memoir, writing, peer editing

OBJECTIVES

Students will:

• Read memoirs and appreciate the narrative elements of people's lives.

• Write memoirs and examine the narrative elements of their own lives.

• Use technology to revise, collaborate, and solicit feedback on their writing.

• Use technology to read, collaborate, and provide feedback on other students' writing.

UNIT DESCRIPTION

This unit can work well with almost any literature or composition course, from ninth grade to graduate school. It is especially successful with reluctant readers, English as a second language (ESL) students, and students entering ninth grade who have special needs.

Many students entering the typical ninth-grade study of genre have difficulty connecting to the short story and will have further difficulty connecting to the novel. This unit uses engaging writing assignments, peer editing, and technology to get students to become better writers and readers. Through collaborative Web sites students write, collect, edit, revise, and comment on memoirs. As students connect experience to writing and appreciate the universal lessons of stories from other people and perspectives, they can become better readers of short stores, novels, and other literature.

TECHNOLOGY

Computers with Internet connections

Online word processing software

SUPPLEMENTARY RESOURCES

For a list of Web resources that is frequently revised and expanded, go to http://del.icio.us/cs272/memoir/.

Resources for Teachers

Composing a Teaching Life (Vinz, 1996)
> A memoir on teaching English that offers insights into memoirs, methods, and the profession of teaching English.

The Reading-Spelling Connection: www.trelease-on-reading.com/spelling-krashen.html
> A source of useful research and methods for improving student writing and reading.

Time for Meaning: Crafting Literate Lives in Middle & High School (Bomer, 1995)
> An engaging and candid account of Randy Bomer's successful methods for teaching writing by connecting students to the process.

Type and Travel: Web-Based Word Processors: http://reviews.cnet.com/4520-9239_7-6627472.html
> A review of Web-based word processors.

Resources for Teachers and Students

Memoirs and Teen Writing Books

Anne Frank: The Diary of a Young Girl (Frank, 1947)

Chicken Soup for the Teenage Soul (Canfield, Hansen, Kirberger, & Claspy, 1997)

I Know Why the Caged Bird Sings (Angelou, 1969)

Narrative of the Life of Frederick Douglass, an American Slave (Douglass, 1845)

Teen Ink: Our Voices, Our Visions (Meyer & Meyer, 2000)

Warriors Don't Cry: A Searing Memoir of the Battle to Integrate Little Rock's Central High (Beals, 1994)

When I Was Puerto Rican (Santiago, 1994)

Teen Writing Web Site

Teen Ink: www.teenink.com
> Web and print outlet for teen writing.

Online Word Processing Programs

Google Documents (formerly Writely): http://docs.google.com

Thinkfree: www.thinkfree.com

Zoho Writer: www.zoho.com

ACTIVITIES

DAYS 1–5

Students begin by reading memoirs and brainstorming ideas.

It is tempting to begin this unit by having students write down some initial drafts of funny, exciting, or interesting experiences in their lives. Having done it that way, I have found this unit to be more successful when students first listen to and read short, engaging memoirs from other teens. Depending on your students, curriculum, and resources you can get these from a variety of sources.

I have been especially successful when beginning with selected stories from the series *Chicken Soup for the Teenage Soul* (Canfield, Hansen, Kirberger, & Claspy). I have to admit, also, that teaching these books was a bit of a risk. Other English teachers in my school were concerned about their appropriateness for the high school English curriculum. However, the use of these popular books was prompted by the blank stares and apathetic readers and writers I had faced the previous year. I will say that beginning with these stories—selecting a variety to read in class and assign for homework—was an unqualified success with both reluctant readers and more advanced students.

There are collections of shorter memoirs and book-length memoirs that you can begin with as well as numerous volumes in the *Chicken Soup for the Teenage Soul* series. Works that you could consider are *When I Was Puerto Rican* (Santiago), *Anne Frank: The Diary of a Young Girl* (Frank), *I Know Why the Caged Bird Sings* (Angelou), *Teen Ink: Our Voices, Our Visions* (Meyer & Meyer), *Warriors Don't Cry: A Searing Memoir of the Battle to Integrate Little Rock's Central High* (Beals), and *Narrative of the Life of Frederick Douglass, an American Slave* (Douglass).

For the stories, episodes, or chapters, call students' attention to the beginnings, story arcs, endings, and interesting features. These will be elements that they will apply in their own writing. Most students come to school with an instinct for story and narrative, so this should be an engaging process.

After you have read and discussed several stories (or if you are using a book-length memoir, several chapters), you will begin the memoir-writing process. First ask students to think about stories from their lives that are funny, sad, interesting, or exciting. They can also write about an interesting routine or ritual that they or their families have.

The story should have a beginning, middle, and end; you can vary the length requirement based on your curriculum and knowledge of your students. You will have them write a collection of memoirs (four to five in all), so you should begin with a shorter length requirement for this first one and then increase the length requirements as the unit progresses.

Ask the students to write down three ideas for memoirs (using Handout 5.1). This should be done at home, so students can reflect and brainstorm without much time pressure. Each student will soon share these ideas in class. It is important to emphasize to students that they will share their stories with others—in and outside the class. This will inform them about revealing information that they might feel should be private or confidential. For some students, thinking of a title is easier and more productive than thinking of a topic. Giving them a choice can stimulate their writing.

DAYS 6–7

Students are introduced to online word processing software and choose an idea for their first memoir.

During these two days you will have the students share their ideas with the class orally and put them online for you and their peer-editing partners. You could have the students share their ideas online with the entire class and do the discussion online. However, this could become a rather cumbersome use of the technology, a distant second choice, considering the benefits of a live discussion.

The technology that the students will be using is an online word processing program. Google Documents (http://docs.google.com), Zoho Writer (www.zoho.com), and Thinkfree (www.thinkfree.com) are three popular choices. This unit will focus on Google Documents, but with modifications these activities can be done with any of them.

Place students in pairs for their initial peer editing. I would strongly recommend pairing students with classmates who have similar writing abilities. This way they can give appropriate critiques and feedback in their skill range—moving from their actual writing levels closer to their potential writing levels with the perspective and feedback of a peer reader. It is important to emphasize that their audience will be teens and adults and that they should strive for clarity for both audiences.

The introduction to the online word processing program and its applications should be based on the students' prior knowledge of desktop word processing. You can eventually teach them how to cooperatively revise and edit as they do the work. Have every student sign up for Google Documents or a comparable online word processing program. These programs are free and all a student needs is a valid e-mail address to activate the account.

Have them create a new document with the three ideas that they brainstormed (Figure 6). This will introduce them, in a safe and familiar way, to online word processing. Then have them make their peer editors and you "collaborators" on this document. They do this simply by clicking the "collaborate" tab and entering an e-mail address.

Figure 6. Online word processing program Google Docs. Students post memoir ideas for teachers and other students.

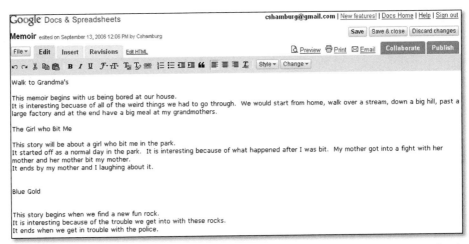

© Google

You will introduce the students to the editing and revision features by having them comment on their partner's ideas. They should state their preference of the three memoirs—which one they would like to learn about. The authors can follow this advice or not when their choose the idea for their first memoir. There will be more memoirs to write, so students can eventually write all three.

The students will get to read these comments on their ideas, and as their memoirs progress, will also be able to see the revision history. The ability for authors and collaborators to review and revert to previous versions is the strength of Google Documents. Using this software, the teacher can track the work of the authors and editors, and the students can work with the comfort of keeping previous versions. Most important, however, students can also see the dynamic give and take of the revision process clearly and powerfully on command. Making revisions and reviewing them are a fundamental component of the unit, and accessing the revision history will be a part of your assessment.

Although document collaboration is possible through e-mail, a school's computer network, or even paper and pen, a Web-based word processing program makes this a seamless, convenient, and accessible process. For all of their other memoirs, students will automatically add both their peer-editing partners and you as collaborators.

DAYS 8–18

Students write their memoirs and collaborate online to peer review each other's work in a structured and supportive process.

This part of the unit focuses on students working collaboratively and the teacher working in writing conferences with each pair. The teacher should take the assessment rubric and review it with each student in discussions of their work. During this time there should be some class discussions on the process and related issues of writing, editing, and memoirs.

In particular, a discussion of genre, conventions, and expectations is important. Memoirs are based on the writer's recollection. Memoir writers do not have the responsibility to verify facts, but they do not have the license to make up narrative elements either. Students should understand that the genre of memoir is considered nonfiction. Memoirs have been used as historic documents (e.g., *Night*, Wiesel) and as medical and psychological case studies (e.g., *Let Me Hear Your Voice*, Maurice). You should also review the controversy over *A Million Little Pieces*, a memoir with fabricated events by the author James Frey. Allowing students to modify their memoirs as fictional works should be an option; however, students should disclose if their works are nonfiction or fiction. Furthermore, you should also discuss the use of pseudonyms to protect the identity of people mentioned in the memoirs. Again, the use of pseudonyms should be disclosed to readers.

By this time, students have brainstormed three ideas and picked one. It is now time for them to complete a first draft of their first memoir. The completion of the first draft begins the peer-editing process. Peer editing can be an extremely productive or frustratingly counter-productive process. Letting students write for an audience, valuing their feedback as readers, and including them in the revision process of another student in a significant way can all lead them to be more invested writers and readers. However, letting students loose with indiscriminate criteria or an overly judgmental mission can quash their initiative as writers, readers, and editors.

The peer-editing process that I propose scaffolds the writers to prepare their work for editing and scaffolds the editors to make useful suggestions to the writers. If you use or modify this model, create your own, or use a different model, I would ask you to keep the following principles in mind. The peer-editing process should be:

- **Supportive.** The students should feel that their work and their feedback are welcome and are valued by the process.

- **Useful.** The process should go beyond a simple collaborative or feel-good experience. The writing itself and the inclination to write should both improve, and students should become better readers and writers.

- **Doable.** The process, handouts, and scaffolding material should give enough guidance so that peer editing can be done in a meaningful way by students. This may mean simplifying the revision process or scaffolding students with a set of expectations and terms for editing.

- **Age and skill appropriate.** The students are expected to improve their writing, not reach or conform to an ideal level of writing. This may mean allowing different styles and even mistakes in final drafts.

My model of the peer-editing process contains the following five elements.

Element 1: Start with a Positive

The peer editor should begin by saying one positive thing about the writing. This sets the tone for both reader and editor that this will be a supportive process.

Element 2: Explain the State of the Draft

Before each submission, the author should tell the editor where this piece is in the process—brainstorm, outline, first draft, second draft, third draft, close to final draft, final draft.

Element 3: Ask Big Questions and Give Big Answers

The author should begin with questions that he wants answered from the editor: Does this have a good opening? Are there enough details? Do I need more descriptions?

The editor should answer these questions. This gives the writer a sense of control and a stronger stake in the process. It prevents the sense of vulnerability that students can feel when submitting personal writing to a teacher or peer editor. These comments can be incorporated into the document or immediately deleted. If others collaborate, edit, or comment, the writer has the ability to see those changes in a different color highlight.

Element 4: Set Standard Terminology for Editors

The editor should use the following four terms and only these terms in the text of the piece—rephrase, expand, move, delete. Each term should then be elaborated on. Giving students a common vocabulary for editing will facilitate the process. Otherwise students might freeze up as editors or hypercriticize the document. These four terms should be distributed to the students and put up on a wall (Handout 5.2).

When you review the revisions of a document, any changes will be highlighted in a different color and correlated to different collaborators. This will continue throughout the revision history of the document. During writing conferences, the teacher and students can review the revision history with dates and see the questions, suggestions, and changes.

Element 5: Take or Ignore the Advice, but Explain the Decisions

It should be emphasized that the writer does not have to follow the peer editor's advice. The teacher's job is to review, in consultation with the writer, each of the drafts, with suggestions made by the peer editor and teacher, and discuss the decisions of the writer— what suggestions were followed and what suggestions were ignored. The writer has to consider the suggestions and explain why they were or were not followed.

Once the first memoir is completed, ask students to choose a new idea to write about. Assign a total of four to five memoirs, and increase the length requirement as you go along. Students will peer edit for their partners, revise their own work, and have conferences with the teacher for each memoir.

Assessment

Writing, particularly memoirs, places students in a vulnerable place. This is true of both skilled and reluctant writers. This unit and the peer-editing process will improve their skills as reader and writers. However, this improvement is not directly correlated to the quality of the final product. Your assessments and teaching should encourage students in the process and not focus on a highly stylized or errorless final product.

As the teacher you should be meeting with groups each day in conferences. During the class periods, students can review their comments, suggestions, and decisions. As you work with each pair of student writers, you can review their progress and their revision process. Distribute and review the rubric early on in the unit. Complete your assessment as you look at each student's work alone and in conferences. Modify and reuse the rubric for each memoir.

Rubric for Memoirs and Online Peer Editing

	Approaches	Meets	Exceeds	Relevant ISTE NETS•S	Relevant IRA/ NCTE Standards
STUDENT AS WRITER					
Submits three ideas online	Three ideas are not submitted	Three ideas are submitted	Three ideas are submitted, each describing a separate and unique episode	1, 2, 4, 5, 6	4, 5, 6, 11, 12
Submits first draft online	First draft is not submitted, OR does not meet length requirement, OR lacks beginning, middle, or end	First draft is submitted, meets length requirement, and has beginning, middle, and end	First draft is submitted, meets length requirement, and has beginning, middle, and end. Concern for expression and maintaining audience interest is clearly demonstrated	1, 2, 4, 5, 6	4, 5, 6, 11, 12
Poses questions online	irrelevant or no questions are posed by author	Significant questions are posed by author	Significant questions are posed by author on the style and content of the work	1, 2, 4, 6	4, 5, 6, 8, 11, 12
Makes subsequent revisions *(in collaboration with peer editor and teacher)*	Author ignores all or most feedback	Author responds to some feedback	Author responds to all or most feedback either by making changes or explaining why changes were not made	1, 2, 4, 5, 6	4, 5, 6, 8, 11, 12
STUDENT AS EDITOR					
Addresses main questions online	Ignores or insufficiently addresses author's questions	Addresses all or most of author's questions	Substantively addresses all of author's questions	2, 4, 5, 6	1, 2, 3, 4, 5, 6, 8, 11
Provides editorial suggestions: rephrase, expand, move, delete	Provides minimal or no editorial suggestions	Provides editorial suggestions with some explanations that make the memoir more interesting and engaging	Provides significant and thoughtful editorial suggestions with clear and logical explanations that make the memoir more interesting and engaging	2, 4, 5, 6	1, 2, 3, 4, 5, 6, 8, 11
Maintains supportive editing tone online	Does not encourage work of writer	Encourages work of writer	Substantively and intelligently encourages work of writer	2, 5	4, 5, 6, 11

A Document in Madness
Teaching "The Yellow Wallpaper" through Video

by Kate Mazzetti

STANDARDS

ISTE NETS for Students	1, 2, 3, 4
IRA/NCTE Standards	1, 2, 3, 4, 5, 6, 11

KEYWORDS

video, Yellow Wallpaper, short story, filmmakers

OBJECTIVES

Students will:

- Read a text closely and make creative decisions in the medium of video.

- Collaborate in groups on specific artistic elements to develop a video.

- Evaluate and provide feedback on all of the components of video production.

- Create an original video version of a text.

UNIT DESCRIPTION

> "The front pattern *does* move—and no wonder! The woman behind shakes it! And she is all the time trying to climb through. But nobody could climb through that pattern—it strangles so …" —Charlotte Perkins Gilman, "The Yellow Wallpaper"

In this project, your students experience literature in an engaging manner by creating a video. It gives them control over their learning in a way that makes them want to work harder and understand the literature on many levels. The medium of video lends itself to many interpretations and allow students to learn on a visceral level. This project can work with a variety of short stories, as well as parts of plays. I have done similar projects on portions of *Hamlet* and *The Crucible*, but this one is unique in that the students not only act and direct, but write the screenplay based on the text itself. Your students will realize that literature can be alive and engaging and that they can bring their own voices to what they are reading. In addition, this project has many facets, thereby engaging the interests of all your students.

The late 19th-century short story "The Yellow Wallpaper," by Charlotte Perkins Gilman, about a woman's "descent into madness" has been heralded as a feminist work. This was a reason of mine for choosing it, as I taught in an all-girls high school. Its themes, however, are relevant for both boys and girls, and can spark discussions on topics such as marital dynamics and gender roles, treatment and mistreatment of neurological issues, as well as creativity and its importance for the mind. The varying interpretations, namely of the main character's "madness," also make this story an interesting one for classes to analyze through this project. The main character, very often called "the narrator" because of her lack of a given name in the story, is prescribed the "rest cure" by physicians "of high standing" (namely her husband and brother) after she has had her baby. The reader is unsure of the initial reasons for this prescription: depression, postpartum issues, or other problems. She is not allowed (per doctors' orders) to write, care for her baby, or engage normally in her existence; rather, she is to lie in bed and "rest." She is infantilized by her husband, who thinks she needs this rest for her own sanity. The irony lies right here: this "rest" is what worsens her mental condition.

The room she is resigned to, in a "vacation home," has yellow wallpaper with outlandish patterns on it. The ensuing outcome of her solitary confinement is her vision of a woman inside the wallpaper. It becomes her mission to release this woman from the wallpaper, and she spends the remainder of the story devising methods to do so. This woman in the wall is representative of herself, and she does "free" her in the end. The issues in the story are rife with fodder for your students: Does the narrator really go mad? Is this "release" of the woman in the wallpaper emblematic of a release from the confinement of her own life, or has she become the ultimate prisoner? What questions arise regarding the diagnosis of females by the at one time all-male neurological profession? What questions arise regarding male-female roles in marriage? Would the narrator have become "better" simply by engaging in her life as a mother, writer, and wife? Students can explore these questions, as well as others, throughout their discussion of the story and preparation for creating the video.

I begin the project with a discussion of the story—its characters and themes. The outcome, however, is far more profound than the ability for students to place facts about the story on paper. Rather, their understanding of the story's nuances come alive as they prepare, rehearse for, and film their final project. Students will, in groups, write the screenplay, act, direct, design the set, and film their video. They should come prepared to work as an ensemble to create this project. Even those who are reluctant to play a dramatic role will have a place in the production. In fact, one of the beauties of the project is the number of elements that the students can become engaged in. Students can also decide to give an area a try that they have perhaps always been interested in, but were never given the opportunity to explore.

This project was done with an inexpensive video camera (purchased used on eBay for $51.98). Appendix B has advice and directions for using digital video, digital storytelling techniques, and desktop video-editing software.

TECHNOLOGY

a computer

a video camera

word processing software

music (CDs or MP3s)

video-editing software (optional)

SUPPLEMENTARY RESOURCES

There are two recommended Web sites that students can consult before the project. The one that includes "Why I Wrote *The Yellow Wallpaper*" is particularly interesting because it gives students an idea of what the writer herself was trying to convey through her work. Online text versions of the story are available, but I found it easier to have each student use a paperback version. Many versions are available; I used the Dover Thrift Edition, which is available for $1.00 a copy. The students can make notes in their copies prior to the project, which can then be brought into groups for discussion.

Charlotte Perkins Gilman, "Why I Wrote *The Yellow Wallpaper*" (1913): www.library.csi.cuny.edu/dept/history/lavender/whyyw.html

Page by Page Books: "The Yellow Wallpaper": www.pagebypagebooks.com

Charlotte_Perkins_Gilman/The_Yellow_Wallpaper/The_Yellow_Wallpaper_p1.html
Full text version of the story online.

"The Yellow Wallpaper" (Gilman, 1892)
Paper version available through Dover Thrift Editions for $1.00.

ACTIVITIES

DAYS 1–2

Discuss "The Yellow Wallpaper" and introduce the video project.

After the students have read the short story for homework, begin discussion of the story, paying particular attention to character analysis, namely of the main character, the narrator. I like to get the students' impressions of the setting, character dynamics (mostly between the narrator and her husband), and the themes that resonate today. Discuss the notion of the "rest cure" and if there are any modern equivalents to it. Also explore the importance of perspectives, as the narrator's life outside the confines of her room is framed by the men in the story. More recent books or films such as *Girl, Interrupted*, by Susanna Kaysen, can be mentioned to make contemporary connections about the treatment of females by the psychiatric profession.

Many points of the story can also be brought up throughout the working of the project: all discussion does not take place on days 1 and 2. The strength of this project lies in student collaboration and what they bring to the story. At the end of day 2, I begin to discuss the project itself. I give the students an evening to think about the role each would like to play, and on day 3 decisions are made. Also have a preliminary discussion on the set and costumes. Because of budget constraints, we did not try to recreate the time period through set and costumes. It adds an interesting element when students are allowed to bring their modern sensibilities to this 19th-century story.

DAY 3

Students form groups based on their role in the video project.

On day 3, you'll divide the class into groups: script writing, acting, set and costume, directing, and camera. Have students state their preference for the area they would like to work in, but let them know that each student may not get his or her first choice, because every area needs to be covered. It may be useful to create a sheet for each student to fill out for his or her first, second, and third choices. This allows the students to have their interests validated, but gives the flexibility to create balanced groups and work on skills that particular students would need. As you plan the groups, you may find that you need to double- or triple-up the acting roles, depending on class size. This can indeed work well, even though there is inconsistency in filming. It is very interesting to see different actors' interpretations during the process.

Once the groups are decided, have students break into them to begin a rudimentary discussion of ideas. Distribute Handouts 6.1–6.5 to the groups. Each member of each group should receive a handout pertaining to that group. Each handout outlines the group's requirements, recommendations, and expectations. Explain the rubric to students so that everything is clear prior to their starting work.

DAYS 4–11

Students plan, film, and wrap up the project.

The groups can spend one to two class periods working on the formulation of ideas for their part of the project. Once the script has been created and has been approved by you, copies can be made and distributed to the actors. It is then each group's responsibility to spend subsequent class periods (two to three) working on creating a set, making directing decisions, and holding rehearsals before filming begins. It is up to you to decide how long you want to spend on the project as a whole. I had the students use three class periods for creating and preparing, three to four for filming, and one for viewing the finished product and holding a wrap-up discussion.

Homework consists of the students in each group working on whatever they need to in order to prepare for the next day. Each student is required to participate, and as the rehearsal process goes on, you can keep track of who in your class is taking part in which part of the project.

Each group should have at least one liaison to each of the other groups. The liaison's job is to talk to the other groups to find out what their direction and progress is and to report back. Then, the liaison is responsible for bringing suggestions to the other group. In this way, there is a formal process to include all students in all aspects of production (see Handout 6.6).

The decision of where to film is your own. I used our school auditorium: large in size and easily available for our use. If you do not have the use of such a large space, the classroom is fine. The scope of the project is not as important as the project itself. Because, as mentioned before, the majority of the action takes place in the narrator's bedroom, it is easy to use a small space as well as a large one.

The remainder of the project, the filming itself, should be a time when you can stand back, be a "guide on the side," and let the students take over. I used a very low-tech video camera in my classes for this project. It is your decision how sophisticated you want to get with editing: you know your budget and school facilities. I actually was happy that our finished product did not look so perfectly "finished," the unmistakable sign of an authentic student project. The students knew when to "cut" filming, and knew their sequence of filming, so there was really no need for any real editing on our part.

It's simple to film each part separately, and in order:

1. Opening credits or just the title (made on computer or on a roll of paper held up by students)

2. Body of the video

3. Closing credits

The students may, and should, incorporate music into the video. The songs that students use should capture the themes of the story.

If each group works well together within the group, as well as with other groups, the project will turn out beautifully. I watched in awe as my students created their videos. By allowing them to take ownership of the work through an active medium such as this, they internalize the literature and find their own voices through it.

Assessment

The important elements of this project are that every student is involved and that students develop a sense that the success of the class is also a personal success. I understand when students are in groups that it is very easy for the "loudest" students to be in the forefront. These values—the participation of every student and the focus on the class's success—are embedded in the tasks and in the assessment.

Use a separate rubric for each group. Complete it as you work with, observe, and hold conferences with each group. Share the rubric with your students before you begin the project.

Rubric for Teaching "The Yellow Wallpaper" through Video

	Approaches	Meets	Exceeds	Relevant ISTE NETS•S	Relevant IRA/NCTE Standards
Vision and evidence	Creative and artistic decisions have little or no correlation with the text	Creative and artistic decisions correlate with evidence from the text	Creative and artistic decisions demonstrate a credible and innovative approach to the text	1, 3, 4	1, 2, 3, 4, 5, 6, 11
Group collaboration	Few group members actively participate in decisions and execution	Most or all group members actively participate in decisions and execution	All group members actively participate in decisions and execution, and are encouraged by each other to participate. Each student encourages all other students to participate	2	1, 2, 3, 4, 5, 6, 11
Class collaboration	Group shows little or no interest in gathering information or providing feedback to other groups	Group engages with most other groups to gather information and provide feedback	Group takes an active and engaged interest in the activities and success of all other groups, gathering valuable information and providing substantial feedback	2	1, 2, 3, 4, 5, 6, 11
Execution	Little effort or care is demonstrated in the execution of the group's tasks	Effort and care are demonstrated in the execution of the group's tasks	Effort and care are demonstrated by all group members in the execution of the group's tasks and in the successful execution of the tasks of all groups	1, 2, 3, 4	1, 2, 3, 4, 5, 6, 11

Audio Interviews for Perspective and Analysis

Figure 7. Microphone
(Image by Duchamp, Creative Commons
Attribution License 2.0)

STANDARDS

ISTE NETS for Students	1, 2, 3, 4, 5, 6
NCTE/IRA Standards	1, 2, 3, 4, 5, 6, 7, 9, 11

KEYWORDS

audio, novels, plays, multiple perspectives, literary analysis, creative writing, *Of Mice and Men*

OBJECTIVES

Students will:

- Build an understanding of text, character, and literary interpretation.

- Integrate historical research with primary texts to create original works.

- Apply technology to create, share, and critique responses to literature.

- Analyze characters in a literary work through a coherent framework of text, personal experience, and historical context.

- Listen to and thoughtfully respond to nonprint texts of other students.

UNIT DESCRIPTION

This lesson combines literary appreciation, creative writing, and historical study, and it correlates with current trends in literary analysis that focus on examining the perspectives of historically marginalized voices. It also gets students reading, writing, and speaking in meaningful and collaborative ways. Students take a character in a novel or short story and create an audio interview of that character. This interview is based on the major decisions and actions of the character. The students combine a close study of the text, historical research, creative writing, and dramatic reading techniques. They work collaboratively on the script and with audio technologies to create the interviews. Through a carefully designed approach, students focus on a variety of perspectives, motives, and decisions for both major and minor characters. Furthermore, the digital recordings of the interviews later become nonprint texts of the class, the material for further sharing and study.

This unit helps students deeply examine characters in a novel or play, even those who are marginalized or strongly defined by other characters in the story. It coincides with current trends in literary analysis to bring context and perspectives to bear on texts. Curley's wife in *Of Mice and Men*, Blanche Dubois in *A Streetcar Named Desire*, and George Murchison in *A Raisin in the Sun* are three examples of characters who rarely elicit empathy or deep consideration from student readers. The character interview is designed to help students understand—though not necessarily agree with—the motives and perspectives of many characters. There are several ways to do this project with and without technology. This project draws from Erick Gordon's (2000) unit, "Occupying Spaces: The Mockingbird Monologues." Gordon's project has students assigned to different characters in *To Kill a Mockingbird*. Through a series of writing prompts they develop a monologue that explains the character's role in the book.

The unit described here specifically focuses on John Steinbeck's novel *Of Mice and Men*, but other works of literature can be used as well.

TECHNOLOGY

Audacity audio-editing software

Internet

MP3 files

SUPPLEMENTARY RESOURCES

For a list of Web resources that is frequently revised and expanded, go to http://del.icio.us/cs272/audio/.

Resources for Teachers

"Occupying Spaces: The Mockingbird Monologues" in *Becoming (Other)wise: Enhancing Critical Reading Perspectives* (Gordon, 2000)
An excellent description of an unit to engage students in character empathy.

Web English Teacher: www.webenglishteacher.com/steinbeck.html
A list of resources for teaching Steinbeck.

Resources for Teachers and Students

Fires in the Mirror (Deavere-Smith, 1992)
The play is based on interviews of people who experienced the Crown Heights riots in New York in 1991. It is also available on audiocassette and VHS.

The First Measured Century: www.pbs.org/fmc/downloadbook.htm
Book (Caplow, Hicks, & Wattenberg), video, and teacher's guide all available through PBS at this Web site. This has some excellent ideas and resources for students' work on contextual material.

The Great Depression (A&E, 1998)

An engaging documentary on all aspects of the great depression. There is a special section on Upton Sinclair's run for the governorship of California that is relevant to this project.

Interviewing for Radio (Beaman, 2000)

A book on formats and techniques for radio interviews.

Of Mice and Men (Steinbeck, 1937)

Sample Audio Interviews for Models and Discussion

The Leonard Lopate Show: www.wnyc.org/shows/lopate/episodes/2006/08/15

Leonard Lopate interviews Ray LeMoine and Jeff Neumann on their experiences driving a bus in Afghanistan.

PRX (Public Radio Exchange): www.prx.org/pieces/5256/

Shantaye Wonzer interviews her mother in "A Foster Care Teen Talks with Her Biological Mom." This interview has some innovative editing techniques and an example of multiple perspectives of an event.

SF Gate: http://cdn.sfgate.com/blogs/sounds/sfgate/chroncast/TechTalk-Apple-Wozniak.mp3

San Francisco Chronicle reporter Matthew Yi interviews Steven Wozniak, one of the founders of Apple.

Audio and Video Interviews

60 Minutes: www.cbsnews.com/sections/60minutes/main3415.shtml

Charlie Rose: www.charlierose.com/ or www.audible.com/charlierose/

Fresh Air: www.npr.org/templates/rundowns/rundown.php?prgId=13

ACTIVITIES

Students work in pairs to get material from the text about their characters.

DAYS 1–3

Assign pairs of students to the following characters in *Of Mice and Men*:

- Lennie

- George

- Curley

- Curley's wife

- Slim

- Crooks

- Swamper

You should give a character to more than one pair of students. Because the pairs will interpret the characters differently, the class receives a richer understanding of literary interpretation.

Have the pairs work on gathering evidence from the text (using Handout 7.1). This activity scaffolds the students in doing textual and primary source research. The students look for four key elements: (1) what the narrator says about a character, (2) what a character says about himself or herself, (3) what others say about a character, and (4) the major decisions and actions that character takes. During this initial period, students should also listen to a variety of interviews, at home or in class. You can choose these from the Sample Audio Interviews for Models and Discussion list in the Supplementary Resources section. You can get additional audio and video interviews from the Audio and Video Interviews list.

For example, if a pair of students is working on Curley's wife, they would complete Handout 7.1. They would get citations and quotes about what the narrator says about the character, what the character says about herself, and what others say about the character. They might then conclude that the three big decisions that Curley's wife makes are:

1. She marries Curley.

2. She talks to Lennie and George when they arrive.

3. She talks to Lennie after he fights Curley.

Based on the quotes and decisions they write down in Handout 7.1, the pair constructs questions and answers for the character interview (Handout 7.2). This will be the work of the next three days.

DAYS 4–6

Students write the interview scripts and explore the motivations and context of their characters' decisions.

Students will then take the research from their text and write an interview script. There should be nine questions—three for each decision: one starter question and two follow-ups. The starter question should ask "why" or "how" about the event. In the past, students have generated such starter questions as "Why did you marry Curley?" The two follow-up questions expand, challenge, or contradict the character's answer, such as, "How could you fall in love with a man who you say is 'mean' (p. 72)?"; "The other men say that you are always hanging around the bunkhouse (p. 23). Why do you do that if you are married?"

Students should use Handouts 7.2, 7.3, and 7.4 together. Handout 7.3 contains the rules for the character interviews (e.g., you cannot change facts and you have to add historical context). One rule of note is that you can allow students to contradict *opinions,* but not *facts.* For example, Curley can dispute the impression that he is mean, but not the fact that he works on a ranch. Often, there will be a gray area between fact and opinion (e.g., Curley is described as a "little guy." Is this a fact or an opinion?). I would encourage you to lean toward judging close calls as *opinions.* This can lead to a deeper and more analytic reading of the novel. More concrete facts (e.g., when and where a person was) should not be allowed to be refuted. This can spiral the interview into some absurd ends. Because all books, students, and classes are different, you will have to make these judgment calls yourself. Have students include the page numbers as they write their interviews. If the preinterview handouts are done correctly, they will be an excellent reference for students' interview research. Ask students to submit a transcript with the page numbers and a first draft of the recording.

DAYS 7–10

Students record interviews of their characters. They then listen to and respond to other students' work as literary texts.

Students should record the interviews on Audacity or a different audio-editing program (see appendix A) and save it as an MP3 file. This can be done in class, at home, or in a library or computer room. I would recommend setting the limits of the interviews at 8–12 minutes. This is enough time for them to develop substantive questions and answers, but will also discourage them from including excessive content or extraneous details. After you have listened to and assessed the interviews, you can consider returning some or all of them for a second recording or an editing of inappropriate material.

You should compile all the interviews, 14 for a class of 28, and put them on a Web site or burn them on a CD, depending on your classroom technology. This compilation of interviews becomes the "nonprint text" of the classroom. You should then assign each student to listen to two interviews and complete the questions on Handout 7.5.

Assessment

You should distribute and review the interview rubric after you have introduced the project to the students. This is a highly creative project that also addresses research skills, so bring particular attention to the research skills embedded in each rubric item.

You should introduce the listener responses rubric when distributing and discussing Handout 7.5. It is important to emphasize that student-generated content should be referenced and cited with the same diligence as primary and contextual sources.

Rubric for Interview

	Approaches	Meets	Exceeds	Relevant ISTE NETS•S	Relevant IRA/NCTE Standards
Preinterview decisions	Zero or one major decision listed	Two major decisions listed	Three major decisions listed		1, 2, 3, 7
Preinterview resources	Little or some significant information or no page numbers	Substantial amount of significant information with correct page numbers	All or almost all of significant information with correct page numbers		1, 2, 3, 7
Questions and answers *(starters and follow-ups/recorded and transcript)*	Off topic or not important to the character or story	Based on major decisions of the character and uses material from story with reasonable explanations and evidence	Based on major decisions of the character and uses material from story with logical and consistent explanations and evidence	1, 2, 3, 4, 5	3, 4, 5, 6, 9, 11
Rules of interview	Little or no adherence to rules of interview	Generally adheres to most rules of interview	Adheres to all rules of interview	2, 4, 5	3, 4, 5, 6, 9, 11
Audio	Significant parts of interview are inaudible	Most or all of interview is audible	All of interview is clearly audible; appropriate dialects and intonations are used	2, 6	3, 6, 9

Rubric for Listener Responses

	Approaches	Meets	Exceeds	Relevant ISTE NETS·S	Relevant IRA/ NCTE Standards
Rationale	Lack of clear evidence or compelling explanations or simply restates material in audio interview	Uses clear evidence and/or compelling explanations that are not in the audio interview to agree or disagree	Uses clear evidence from text and contextual material (e.g., history text or secondary sources) that are not in the audio interview to agree or disagree	2, 3, 4, 5, 6	1, 2, 3, 4, 6, 11

Work Cited

Gordon, E. (2000). Occupying spaces: The mockingbird monologues. In R. Vinz (Ed.), *Becoming (other)wise: Enhancing critical reading perspectives* (pp. 8–42). Portsmouth, NH: Heinemann.

UNIT 8

Persuasive Communication
Sending a Video to Your Representative

STANDARDS

ISTE NETS for Students   1, 2, 3, 4, 5, 6

IRA/NCTE Standards   1, 2, 3, 4, 5, 6, 7, 8, 11, 12

KEYWORDS

persuasive communication, digital video, digital storytelling, current events, authentic assessment, anchored learning, WebQuests, YouTube, Internet video

OBJECTIVES

Students will:

- Gather and organize credible information using a variety of sources and media.

- Integrate communication technology and persuasive media to address social and political issues.

UNIT DESCRIPTION

In this project, students create a short video or digital story about a national issue and then send it to their representative or senator. The video and appeal to the representative or senator are also made public—for viewing and comment—through video-sharing services such as YouTube (www.youtube.com), TeacherTube (www.teachertube.com), Castpost (www.castpost.com), or Revver (www.revver.com). This motivates and empowers students with a wider audience and increases the influence of their videos. Students can choose a topic in national discourse, or they can propose legislation on an issue that is important, but not prominent (more funding for research on a particular disability, greater awareness of a specific concern, person, or event). Although the topics might differ, the process, product, and evaluation are similar.

This unit is loosely based on the popular technique of a WebQuest. The WebQuest is a format for research projects and has six components: Introduction, Task, Process, Resources, Evaluation, and Conclusion (Dodge, 1997). This unit is only loosely based on the WebQuest because I have noticed a problem with teachers who frequently use the WebQuest template— students have difficulty transferring the research skills beyond the WebQuest assignments.

WebQuests are excellent opportunities to provide anchored projects that scaffold the students in research techniques by providing a selected list or resources. However, too much reliance on the format can impede developing student research skills, and overly contrived tasks can undermine goals associated with learner-centered pedagogies. The task of this project is not just anchored in a scenario that simulates real-world situations as WebQuests should do, but directly connects students to authentic phenomena and situations outside the classroom.

This project can be effective with a variety of digital storytelling software or digital video. Students are given a task, a set of resources, a variety of software options, an assessment, and a time for reflection.

Online video is a powerful force in today's society—it played a mainstream role in presidential politics with the CNN/YouTube primary debates of 2007. It would be irresponsible not to address it with today's students. However, it would also be irresponsible to give impressionable and vulnerable minors an education using online video without caveats and security measures. I would strongly recommend adapting the permission letter from unit 1 if students will have their own accounts. You should particularly emphasize the need to refrain from divulging personally identifying information. I would also strongly recommend monitoring all comments on the students' videos. These comments are public and can all be monitored from one site using an RSS aggregator. You should also require students to report any messages that they receive through the video-sharing Web site's messaging system. Finally, if students have the option of using their own accounts, I would strongly recommend obtaining parental permission.

If student accounts are not used, the teacher could use his or her own account to post the students' videos and then report back to the students about any comments received. When using a single teacher account, all the communication and activity can be monitored by the teacher. If this is the direction that you choose, I would also recommend sharing the gist of all communication with students in a sensitive and developmentally appropriate way. For example, if a profane comment is posted, this can be shared with the students, though not necessarily verbatim, as an illustrative example of abuses on the Web. In this way you avoid giving students a dangerously naïve view of the Internet, but also spare them the blunt realities of inappropriate language and online solicitation.

TECHNOLOGY

    computers with Internet access

    Video-sharing Web sites

    RSS software

Digital Storytelling Software

    GarageBand (Apple)

    iPhoto (Apple)

    Photo Story (Microsoft)

Digital Video-Editing Software

MovieMaker (Microsoft)

iMovie (Apple)

Premier Elements (Adobe)

Premier (Adobe)

ShowBiz DVD (ArcSoft)

Vegas Movie Studio (Sony)

MediaStudio (Ulead)

Please refer to appendix B (on using video).

SUPPLEMENTARY RESOURCES

For lists of Web resources that are frequently revised and expanded, go to http://del.icio.us/cs272/video and http://del.icio.us/representative/.

Resources for Teachers

TechCrunch: www.techcrunch.com/2005/11/06/the-flickrs-of-video/
Overview of the choices and features of video-sharing Web sites.

Resources for Teachers and Students

Idebate Database: www.idebate.org/debatabase/
A resource for student debaters that provides contrasting perspectives on many topical issues. I have found this site to provide balanced perspectives on issues, but please note to yourself and to students that the About page indicates the organization's affiliation with the Open Society Institute (OSI), a part of the Soros Foundation Network, whose Chairman George Soros is a activist in liberal and democratic causes. The OSI has a clear mission to separate itself from the political activities of George Soros (www.soros.org/about/bios/a_soros/political). I have found this to be the case for the Idebate Web site, but this is an important and teachable issue for you and your students.

Opposing Viewpoints (book series edited by William Dudley; online database from Thompson/Gale at www.gale.com/OpposingViewpoints/)
Balanced views on a variety of contemporary topics.

Politics 1: www.politics1.com/issues.htm
A site that attempts to present balanced overviews (liberal and conservative) on contemporary political and social issues.

Thomas at the Library of Congress: http://thomas.loc.gov
Library of Congress site that provides information on recent or pending legislation. Excellent source for ideas about *under-recognized issues* as well as pending legislation on *prominent issues*. Both under-recognized issues and prominent issues are terms used in this unit.

U.S. House of Representatives: www.house.gov
Find your representative's address, e-mail, and Web site. The Web site should contain the representative's positions on most major issues.

U.S. Senate: www.senate.gov
Find your senator's address, e-mail, and Web site. The Web site should contain the senator's positions on most major issues.

Video-Sharing Web Sites

Castpost: www.castpost.com

Google Video: http://video.google.com

Revver: http://ww.revver.com

TeacherTube: http://teachertube.com
Modeled on YouTube, but a focus on educational videos and student projects.

YouTube: www.youtube.com
Note that Google now owns YouTube and the site integrates with Google Video.

ACTIVITIES

DAYS 1–2

Students brainstorm topics for their persuasive video.

The class will brainstorm with the teacher on the two types of issue that can be the subjects of their video. Their task will be to create a video addressed to their representative or senator on an issue in the public discourse (prominent issues such as gun control, abortion, war, foreign aid, oil drilling in the Arctic) or on an issue that should have more national attention (under-recognized issues such as the need for autism awareness, need for increased breast cancer screenings, need to address teen violence, acknowledgment of under-recognized groups such as women in WWII). In groups of three or four, students list four to six possible topics in each category. You can scaffold them by proving examples of each category. Please note that students do not have to take a position on these issues now, just map out the landscape. For each issue, they will develop a concept map that illustrates the major components of each issue as they know them now. Teachers should remind students that this is an initial brainstorming session and that this information is likely to be faulty and incomplete.

DAYS 3–5

Students select their topics and begin their research.

Students pick their topics and begin their research. Student can refer to their brainstorming notes, select topics that were discussed in class, or go in a new direction. They will describe three ideas—prominent issues, under-recognized issues, or a combination of the two—and submit them for your feedback (Handout 8.1). Typically, you will allow a student to work on his or her first topic. However, sometimes the topic is either dated or would not make a substantial research project. Having two others topics that the student is already invested in makes selecting another one easier. If the first topic is not practical, this process also helps students select topics that are both suitable and of interest to them. They can refer to the following three resources for ideas:

- Idebate Database: www.idebate.org/debatabase/
  A resource for student debaters that provides contrasting perspectives on many topical issues.

- Politics 1: www.politics1.com/issues.htm
  This site attempts to present balanced overviews (liberal and conservative) on contemporary political and social issues.

- Thomas at the Library of Congress: http://thomas.loc.gov
  Library of Congress site that provides information on recent or pending legislation. Excellent source for ideas about under-recognized issues as well as pending legislation on prominent issues.

For example, a student might use Idebate for brainstorming (Figure 8). She can type in "United States" and retrieve the following 12 topics.

1. Should the United States ratify the Comprehensive Test Ban Treaty?

2. Should the United States drop its sanctions on Cuba?

3. Should the United States provide debt relief through the UN to countries affected by natural disasters?

4. Should the United States Congress allow drilling for oil in the Arctic National Wildlife Refuge?

5. Should the United States support a global tax?

6. Should the United States or any other State continue to reject the International Criminal Court (ICC)? Is the ICC both dangerous to democracy and doomed to fail?

7. Should the USA discontinue the production of land mines, and sign the Ottawa Convention?

8. Should the United States conduct research into mini-nukes?

9. Should the United States, Canada, and Mexico come together to form a North American Economic and Security Community?

10. Is the United States of America imperialist?

11. Should the United States participate in UN peacekeeping operations and, if so, should the United States permit its troops to serve as UN troops (rather than as U.S. troops under an independent command)?

12. The United States has a policy of making its support to the United Nations conditional on its maintenance of a no-growth budget. This means that the UN must maintain roughly the same bottom line while reprioritizing its spending within those parameters. Should this U.S. policy be changed?

From this list and the brainstorming in class, she might choose to explore the issue of drilling in the Arctic National Wildlife Refuge. Idebate can give her an initial overview of the topic, and she can then research and explore it further. She might have an inclination to either support it or oppose it, and her further research can affirm or confound her expectations. She can also develop persuasive power by knowing and addressing the arguments of her opposing side. Idebate is an excellent starting point for this process.

DAYS 6–10

Students research topics, gather material, and create their videos.

Once the students pick their topics they will research material to create an effective three to five minute video. Conducting research, writing narration, selecting and arranging effective images, and articulating the salient points are processes that dynamically intersect in the creation of an effective video. Use Handouts 8.2 and 8.3 to inform your instruction and guide your students.

Students use Handout 8.2 to organize all the persuasive and informative elements of their presentations. Once students have their topics, they will need to collect supporting evidence and incorporate it with their ideas. This sheet will help them organize the facts, ideas, quotes, and images as well as the main points that they want to emphasize. This is a dynamic process in which a persuasive image might inspire a few sentences of narration, or a necessary fact might require an accompanying image. Students must have a main idea and supporting information and ideas. However, there is no single way to organize the video—the keys are credibility, clarity, and persuasion.

Figure 8.
Idebate Database
(www.idebate.org)

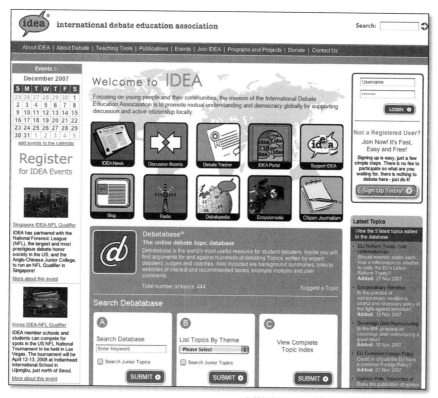

© 2006 International Debate Education Association

Students use Handout 8.3 to organize their video. They will definitely need several pages. This handout is especially useful if you have a limited number of computers or students without computers at home. They can learn the general procedures for creating a video without the software or media. If your students are proficient users of technology or video-editing software, this paper version might slow them down. This is not necessarily a bad thing as it can spur reflection and thought before they use the technology.

DAYS 11–12

Students share their work with classmates, the school, their elected officials, and the world.

When students complete their work and you have assessed it, you might want to consider having a short film festival in your class or school. When the videos have been finalized, you should then prepare them to go public. I would recommend two related methods of dissemination. Students should directly e-mail it to their senator or representative, noting that it will also be made public and providing the URL. At the same time, students should make it public on a video-sharing site such as YouTube. When they do this, it is important that you review the tags or keywords that they will use. This will make it searchable. Once it is up, other people from around the world will be able to view it, rate it, and comment on it. You can set up a RSS feed for each video and track the comments in an RSS aggregator throughout the rest of the school year. Students will see the effect that their video has.

Assessment

This is a long rubric and has the challenging role of isolating distinct skills in a project—a video—that works best as a single, holistic experience. I would strongly recommend distributing and reviewing the rubric early and then referring to it frequently during class and individually with students throughout the project. The items are best understood in the context of doing the project and are excellent guidelines for each step of production.

Rubric for Persuasive Communication

	Approaches	Meets	Exceeds	Relevant ISTE NETS•S	Relevant IRA/ NCTE Standards
NARRATION *(and Text Transcript)*					
Organization	Lacks main idea and/or supporting details and evidence	Main idea presented with supporting details and evidence	Main idea clearly presented and expertly supported with details and evidence	1, 2, 3, 4, 5, 6	1, 2, 3, 4, 5, 7, 8, 11, 12
Use of evidence	Ineffectively uses facts, quotes, and/or interviews	Effectively uses facts, quotes, and/or interviews	Effectively uses facts, quotes, and interviews	2, 3, 4, 5	7, 8
Synchronization	Narration does not correlate to images	Narration appropriately correlates to images	Narration enhances and is enhanced by images and other audio	2, 6	4, 6
Articulation	Narration is not clearly written or is not clearly spoken	Narration in general is clearly written and spoken	Narration is expertly written and spoken	2, 6	4, 6
RESEARCH					
Credibility	Few or no facts or quotes are used or they are from sources without experience or expertise in topic	Many facts and quotes are from sources that have experience or expertise in topic	Most or all facts are from sources that have extensive experience and expertise in topic	3, 4	3, 7, 8
Citation	Little or no citation of sources for facts and interviews	Some citation of sources for facts and interviews	Appropriate citation of sources for facts and interviews effectively incorporated into the narration	2, 3, 5	7, 8

(Continued)

Rubric for Persuasive Communication *(Continued)*

	Approaches	Meets	Exceeds	Relevant ISTE NETS•S	Relevant IRA/ NCTE Standards
IMAGES					
Use of images	Few or no images effectively communicate the purpose of the presentation	Many images effectively communicate the purpose of the presentation	Most or all images effectively communicate the purpose of the presentation	1, 2, 4, 6	4, 6, 8
Documentation of image sources	Image sources are not clearly or consistently documented	Most image sources are clearly and consistently documented	All image sources are clearly and consistently documented at the end of the video	2, 3, 5	4, 8
MEDIA INTEGRATION					
Coordination of images, narration, and audio	Sequence, timing, and transitions are not used effectively or thoughtfully	Sequence, timing, and transitions are generally used effectively and thoughtfully	Sequence, timing, and transitions are consistently used effectively and thoughtfully	1, 2, 6	4, 6, 12
Use of music and other audio	Lack or excess of music and other audio or use is generally indiscriminate	Music and other audio are generally used purposefully and effectively	Music and other audio are used purposefully, effectively, and consistently throughout the video	1, 2, 6	4, 6

Work Cited

Dodge, B. (1997). *Some thoughts about WebQuests*. Retrieved October 17, 2006, from http://Webquest.sdsu.edu/about_Webquests.html

UNIT 9

Technology and the Research Paper

by Yvette Louis

STANDARDS

ISTE NETS for Students   1, 2, 3, 4

IRA/NCTE Standards   1, 2, 3, 4, 5, 6, 7, 8, 9, 10, 11, 12

KEYWORDS

literary research, research databases, library databases, information literacy, Scarlet Letter, In the Blood, Tituba

OBJECTIVES

Students will:

- Increase their independent learning skills.

- Develop research skills and learn holistic research methods.

- Hone their presentation skills.

- Improve their technology literacy and information literacy.

- Develop an inner editor.

- Build literary skills through reading, analyzing, and interpreting literary works.

UNIT DESCRIPTION

Literary research is commonly viewed as an activity that involves gathering carefully cited facts and quotes to support arguments in term papers, separate from reading and from other class activities, and enacted in its own special place, the library. The pressures technology has placed on the classification and movement of knowledge have hastened our realization that the conventional view of research is woefully narrow, that the skills of "active construction and evaluation" (Brent, 1992, n.p.) demanded by research are now required for nearly every communication, making literary research a holistic activity. Just as some students think of research as an inconvenient trip to the library, some instructors think of literary research as unnecessary. Why should students undertake literary research when all they need to do is read the text and respond in written form, perhaps answer some prefabricated questions supplied by the publisher in an expedient separate section? To excise literary research from the classroom is not only to deny students an opportunity to develop mastery over the tools of knowledge, but also to deny the reality that they will need to apply these skills in their quotidian lives in a world increasingly shaped by technology.

What I have termed the holistic research process is active and engaged, not only in every phase of literary interaction, from reading, to writing, to editing, to publishing, but also in writing blogs, voting, deciphering instructions, and becoming astute consumers. Holistic literary research helps students become independent learners, gain confidence in manipulating knowledge daily, place texts in contexts, and develop much-needed perspective by evaluating every piece of knowledge that may cross their path.

Like reading, holistic literary research is most often a solitary activity that paradoxically immerses one in the construction of knowledge. Just as sitting in front of a computer is perceived as an alienating and lonely practice when in reality it has increased social interaction for many through online communities, reading is also perceived as an isolating activity when it actually involves an asynchronous deep communication with others through the text. Similarly, holistic research may appear to be a lonely activity, but in fact it is defined by wide-ranging forms of communication, with self, with content, with others through the knowledge they create and disseminate through various media. As we come in contact with knowledge, we create in turn.

Readers represent the smallest unit of carriers of local knowledge. We bring to the act of reading every bit of knowledge that we have acquired throughout our lives. The process of interacting with the text is a process of invention, of creativity. We are envisioning the content we are reading, framing it within our universe of knowledge, imagining a narrator, and engaging in a plethora of other creative activities. Writing down our thoughts about what we have read is an act of communicating, of producing knowledge, not just of transmitting knowledge from responder to receiver, but of interpreting, weighing, evaluating, supplementing, and sifting. In this very concrete way, "knowledge is socially constructed" (Brent, 1992, n.p.). Literary research immerses readers in the great river of knowledge that flows before them and after them like a vast epistemological genealogical chart. By reading and writing, students are making themselves participants in the stream of knowledge, crossing geographical, temporal, and conceptual boundaries. Without doing the work of literary research, the stream is dammed, the lines of communication are cut, and the conversation becomes one-sided. Holistic research segues between the past and present, communicates through a wide range of narrators and readers, and otherwise constructs pathways that link all areas of our lives in the act of processing and creating knowledge. The holistic approach to literary research asks:

> What does it really mean to search, not just through one's own storehouse of knowledge and values, but through other writers' storehouses, in search of the answer to a question? What does it mean to interpret large numbers of often-conflicting texts, evaluate the opinions expressed, and create from an amalgam of one's own and other people's beliefs a new answer, a new piece of knowledge that is not just a patchwork of sources but an original system of beliefs that could not have existed without the believer's having considered other texts? (Brent, 1992, n.p.)

Even before that visit to the library, the holistic researcher had employed the skills of literary research in reading, note-taking, deciding on topics, and sharing responses to reading with others. After the library, holistic literary research practices continue while formulating a thesis, composing a first draft, writing a bibliography, and returning yet again to sources. Holistic literary research recognizes that knowledge is not handled in a linear fashion, but in a repetitive, circular, and recursive manner. These patterns are facilitated and even necessitated by new technologies.

In the Information Age, research has been subsumed under the broader term *information literacy* for good reason. As information charges upon us at ever-increasing rates, we find ourselves in need of holistic strategies to manage it. According to the American Library Association (2006): "The sheer abundance of information will not in itself create a more informed citizenry without a complementary cluster of abilities necessary to use information effectively" (n.p.). For any of us to stay afloat in the accelerating information stream, we will need to learn to tread critically. Those sophisticated research capabilities that were once considered the purview of scientists, librarians, and esoteric scholars have become the essential tools of every lifelong learner and "information consumer" (The University of Texas System Digital Library, 2004). Clearly information management is no longer limited to issues of data storage. The sooner students develop competencies in information literacy, the better equipped they will be to survive the onrush of data that awaits them.

Information literacy can be thought of as a series of strategies for manipulating knowledge. The National Forum on Information Literacy defines it as "the ability to know when there is a need for information, to be able to identify, locate, evaluate, and effectively use that information for the issue or problem at hand" (Jackman & Weiner, n.d., n.p.). These strategies require the development of knowledge about knowledge, not only applying traditional skills to new media and acquiring new competencies, but manipulating the relationship between them, what Irvin Katz (2005) refers to as *information-handling skills*. Rather than just going to the library for a few hours to work on a paper, this new research process requires "continuous scanning of the environment for information that is relevant to work or personal life" (Steyaert, n.d., n.p.). At every stage of the writing process and indeed, of the learning process, students are required to gauge the reliability of sources, sift through seemingly endless streams of information in various media, judge what is relevant to their needs, and organize information from a variety of sources into coherent narratives, all the while fighting off data overload.

The consequences of information illiteracy are not just limited to scholastic performance. As one Educational Testing Service (ETS) publication states: "It is as if the Internet, in making information accessible and convenient, has paradoxically led to a *decrease* in the critical thinking skills needed to deal with information" (Katz, 2005, p. 8). It has been my experience that many students are not all that familiar with information-gathering tools or even with software applications. Educators and parents often make the mistake of assuming that because students know their way around gadgets and cell phones, that they are computer literate. Information literacy requires critical thinking of the highest order and while it does require basic keyboard, mouse, and reading skills, these do not guarantee clear thinking any more than the simple possession of pen and paper guarantees clear writing. Lest we confuse technology with knowledge, we are reminded that: "Students often can use the technology, but do not think critically when locating, evaluating and processing the information" (Katz, 2005, p. 7). Another researcher, Breivik, warns us that: "What is growing ever more obvious is that today's undergraduates are generally less prepared to do research than were students of earlier generations, despite their familiarity with powerful new information-gathering tools." (as cited in Katz, 2005, p. 8). Overcoming information illiteracy through holistic research suggests that information literacy competencies as well as independent learning strategies be applied at every phase of the writing process.

The step-by-step process of writing has been described using many models that follow a familiar trajectory from idea to publication. Some processes such as editing and thesis rewriting repeat in recursive patterns before the final product is considered finished. What I call the cycle of writing (Figure 9) follows the familiar steps of invention, thesis, draft, research, revision, and publication.

Figure 9.
Cycle of writing

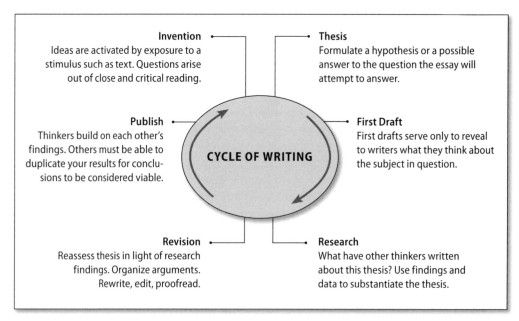

The holistic research process engages competencies of information literacy and student-centered learning practices and makes critical and efficient use of technologies at every stage of the cycle of writing.

Information Literacy Competencies

ETS (2006) has examined information and communication technology (ICT) and proposes a model for developing information literacy that separates competency into seven skill areas: define, access, manage, integrate, evaluate, create, and communicate. Along with the definition of each competency, sample activities that engage each skill accompany the model.

The ETS Model

Define. The ability to use ICT tools to identify and appropriately represent an information need.

Activities include:

- Creating an academic research topic to fit a particular information need
- Asking questions to clarify a customer's information need
- Completing a concept map

Access. The ability to collect and retrieve information in digital environments. This includes the ability to identify likely digital information sources and to get the information from those sources.

Activities include:

- Searching through databases for information
- Browsing through linked Web sites for information
- Locating information through online help tools
- Downloading and installing a (simulated) video player

Manage. The ability to apply an existing organizational or classification scheme for digital information. This ability focuses on reorganizing existing digital information from a single source using existing organizational formats. It includes the ability to identify existing organization schemes, select appropriate schemes for the current usage, and apply the schemes.

Activities include:

- Sorting e-mails into appropriate folders
- Re-ordering a table to maximize efficiency in two tasks with incompatible requirements
- Documenting relationships using an organization chart

Integrate. The ability to interpret and represent digital information. This includes the ability to use ICT tools to synthesize, summarize, compare, and contrast information from multiple digital sources.

Activities include:

- Synthesizing information from IMs into a word-processing document
- Comparing and contrasting information from Web pages in a spreadsheet

Evaluate. The ability to determine the degree to which digital information satisfies the needs of the task in ICT environments. This includes the ability to judge the quality, relevance, authority, point of view/bias, currency, coverage, or accuracy of digital information.

Activities include:

* Selecting the best database for an information need

* Determining the sufficiency (or lack) of information in a Web site, given the information need

* Ranking Web pages in terms of meeting particular criteria

* Determining the relevance of postings on a Web discussion board

Create. The ability to generate information by adapting, applying, designing, or inventing information in ICT environments.

Activities include:

* Creating a graph that supports a point of view

* Selecting text and graphics that support a point of view

Communicate. The ability to communicate information properly in its context of use for ICT environments. This includes the ability to gear electronic information for a particular audience and to communicate knowledge in the appropriate venue.

Activities include:

* Formatting a word-processing document

* Recasting an e-mail

* Adapting presentation slides

* Preparing a text message for a cell phone

© Educational Testing Service

Notice that all the activities can be identified as those required for conducting holistic research. Some demand minimal uses of electronic or digital technology and others call for sophisticated practical knowledge of computer applications. All of the activities, however, presuppose the exercise of critical-thinking skills upon a variety of data across various forms of media. The trademarked Big6 Skills Model (Eisenberg, 2003) proposes a slightly different version of information literacy that isolates six competencies: task definition, information-seeking strategies, location and access, use of information, synthesis, and evaluation. Both the ETS and the Big6 model achieve similar ends by slightly different means, and they are both useful as guides for planning lessons, curricula, and learning activities.

While both models present competencies in a linear fashion for the sake of explanation, in real-life research, all of these isolated tasks are engaged simultaneously in complex ways that would be very difficult to map out and impossible to articulate in a linear fashion. Rebecca Moore Howard (2006) emphasizes the multifaceted aspect of holistic research, asserting that

> the research process today is fundamentally rhizomatic. Information-seeking in new media goes in multiple unplanned directions simultaneously, and it is from these disparate, sometimes unconnected threads that researchers make meaning. Everything we teach about research in our classes—graduate as well as undergraduate—is rendered useless unless we can address these and other challenges of contemporary information literacy. (n.p.)

I would add that the rhizome needs to be dynamic and tentacular, constantly adapting to the tasks of seeking, judging, gathering, sorting, and organizing information.

Both models demand more active participation on the part of the student and fluency in many more types of media, categories of data, and technologies over a longer period. Holistic research will require that students carry out many of its tasks independently as they encounter information from sources outside the classroom and away from the supervision of their instructors. Seeking, judging, gathering, sorting, and organizing information independently becomes essential in holistic research. Yet independence is one of the most challenging characteristics to foster in the classroom. Traditional classroom practices have not focused on nurturing independence, and both students and instructors are suffering from the growing pains of being forced to let go of the dependency of the past. Incorporating student-centered pedagogical practices is one way to meet the challenge and to encourage independent thinking and learning practices.

Student-Centered Learning Principles

Student-centered learning (SCL) provides a paradigm for encouraging independent learning. Motivated by research articles on SCL (O'Neill, Moore, & McMullin, 2005), several years ago I made a full leap into SCL practices in the classroom and have been inspired by its success. Students in all my courses are involved at the "stage when the task is set" and involved "at the stage after the task is completed," including designing syllabi, selecting readings, choosing and setting assessment criteria, designing tasks and learning activities, engaging in self- and peer-assessment, and grading themselves. In the first weeks of the semester we discuss SCL at length and incorporate the following principles and characteristics of SCL as outlined by Brandes and Ginnis (as cited in O'Neill et al., 2005) into the course planning:

- The learner has full responsibility for her/his learning
- Involvement and participation are necessary for learning
- The relationship between learners is more equal, promoting growth, development
- The teacher becomes a facilitator and resource person
- The learner experiences confluence in his education (affective and cognitive domains flow together)
- The learner sees himself differently as a result of the learning experience (n.p.)

The more I work with SCL as a pedagogical practice, the better results I observe in the classroom as a result of its application. Students are challenged to take responsibility for their learning experience. While there may be some disbelief, confusion, and sometimes resistance to SCL practices at the beginning of the semester, once students get over the learning curve, I have found that students are more engaged with the act of learning as well as with the material. The practice of owning their learning experience results in greater confidence in their skills. When students are expected to assume responsibility for their learning, independent thinking is encouraged. Some strategies for implementing student-centered learning include involving students in planning courses, designing syllabi, scheduling and designing learning activities, choosing topics for presentations and papers, creating original theses for papers and presentations, evaluating and designing assessments, scheduling assessments, and editing themselves and peers. Even if only one or two of these activities are introduced to lessons, involving students in creating learning tasks can help them take more responsibility, feel greater ownership of their learning process, and gain some much-needed perspective on education. Students involved to this degree in the creation and execution of learning activities often remark that they gain a new appreciation for teaching. Most important, these habits of independence are transferable to the holistic research process.

The Holistic Research Process and Technology

The holistic research process is characterized as the dynamic incorporation of information literacy competencies, student-centered learning practices, and technology into the cycle of writing. Contrary to the popular opinion that technology is alienating, I have been delighted to observe that incorporating technology ensures that each student is engaged with the material. For example, students who are shy about speaking in class will express themselves more freely in group discussions whether in class or online. As students get to know each other in the small group and discussion forum environment and work together in teams to overcome the challenges of learning new technologies, their comfort level increases and extends to the general classroom discussion and enriches face-to-face conversations. This helps establish a framework of trust that is absolutely necessary for the delicate task of peer editing that comes later in the cycle of writing.

It might seem contradictory to discuss low-tech options in a book about learning and technology, but I discourage the use of technology for its own sake. As with any tool, it's not the technology itself that is responsible for outcomes, but its application. It is the people who apply the technology to inventive ends that produce benefits. The application of these technologies in individual teaching and learning situations also needs to be constantly assessed. And when we experience the occasional technological glitch, it is helpful to have low-tech options prepared and ready to pull out of our pedagogical bag of tricks.

The Activities section incorporates information literacy and student-centered learning into a writing cycle that engages holistic research practices. Do not try to incorporate everything in one class. Start slowly. Become familiar with one aspect of information literacy or student-centered learning or one new research practice and technology and test it on one class for one term. Once you have identified what works and what doesn't and have mastered that particular component, take on another one. You will be surprised by how quickly cumulative changes become apparent in the learning environment. An instructor who models the behavior that is being taught makes an impression. To that end, know that effective instructors are themselves independent learners who seek information; locate, identify, evaluate, document, and apply sources during lectures and in lesson plans; and are constantly modeling best practices in uses of technology.

TECHNOLOGY

Microsoft PowerPoint

Microsoft Word

Adobe Acrobat or Reader for Portable Document Format (PDF) documents

Computer with Internet access

Course Management Systems (Moodle, WebCT, Blackboard)

SmartBoards

Projector (optional)

SUPPLEMENTARY RESOURCES

Primary Texts

The Scarlet Letter (Hawthorne, 1850)

I, Tituba: Black Witch of Salem (Condé, published in 1986, translated into English in 1992)

In the Blood (Parks, first produced in 1999, published in 2000)

Research Tools

Amazon.com: www.amazon.com

Google: www.google.com

Wikipedia: www.wikipedia.org

Literary Databases

The following literary electronic databases are useful for literary research and available through libraries.

Academic Search Premier: www.ebsco.com/home/

JSTOR: The Scholarly Journal Archive: www.jstor.org

Modern Language Association (MLA): www.mla.org
    The MLA bibliography is the core of literary research. The Web site offers information on MLA publications and the MLA bibliography.

Literature Online

For full text and articles through libraries only.

Books in Print: www.booksinprint.com/bip/

The New York Public Library: www.nypl.org

Wilson OmniFile Full Text, Mega Edition: www.hwwilson.com/Databases/omnifile.htm

General Research

Oxford English Dictionary (OED) is good for etymologies. OED Online (subscription service): www.oed.com

Consult LexisNexis *Academic* for newspapers, periodicals, current affairs, and reviews. LexisNexis *Academic* (subscription service): http://academic.lexisnexis.com

Literary Research

How to Write a Term Paper (Gale Cengage Learning): www.gale.com/free_resources/term_paper/index.htm

Library of Congress Research Tools: www.loc.gov/rr/tools.html

Information Literacy

American Library Association: www.ala.org/acrl/ilcomstan.html
> I highly recommend the American Library Association's Web site, which covers information literacy standards. Their extremely detailed and logically structured document also includes suggested model activities and can be used for course planning. This Web address takes you directly to the Information Literacy Competency Standards for Higher Education.

The Big6 Skills Model: www.big6.com/showarticle.php?id=16
> Eisenberg's model isolates six competencies: task definition, information-seeking strategies, location and access, use of information, synthesis, and evaluation.

New Jersey City University (NJCU), Information Literacy Tutorial: www.njcu.edu/Guarini/Instructions/ILTutorial/ILTutorial.htm
> NJCU's library provides extensive tools for identifying information literacy skills and for incorporating activities that develop information literacy in the classroom.

Texas Information Literacy Tutorial (TILT): http://tilt.lib.utsystem.edu/intro/misconceptions.htm

Student-Centered Learning

Emerging Issues in the Practice of University Learning and Teaching: www.aishe.org/readings/
> Geraldine O'Neill, Sarah Moore, and Barry McMullin are the editors of this publication by the All Ireland Society for Higher Education (AISHE).

Online References

Bartleby.com: Great Books Online: www.bartleby.com
> Extensive reference materials, including *The Elements of Style*, by William Strunk Jr. and E. B. White.

Copyright.com: www.copyright.com
> Detailed information about compliance services and guidance on when and how to obtain copyright permissions. Access to educational resources, such as the Campus Guide to Copyright Compliance and Guide to E-Reserve Best Practices.

Dictionary.com: www.dictionary.com

Hypertext Sources

Electronic Literature Directory: http://directory.eliterature.org

PennSound, Center for Programs in Contemporary Writing at the University of Pennsylvania: www.writing.upenn.edu/pennsound/

Poets.org: www.poets.org
> The Academy of American Poets, the largest organization in the country dedicated specifically to the art of poetry, currently features biographies of more than 500 poets, with new pages being added all the time.

Online eText Sources

Project Gutenberg: www.Gutenberg.org
> The site offers 19,000 free books in about 50 languages at this writing, including texts by canonical writers.

Bartleby.com: Great Books Online: www.bartleby.com
> Wide range of primary texts as varied as Homer's *Odyssey*, Cervantes's *Don Quixote*, Nathaniel Hawthorne's *The Scarlet Letter*, and the *Oxford Shakespeare*.

ACTIVITIES

The following primary texts are the focal point of this unit. They should be read in chrono-logical order. Readings may be supplemented by various musical and cinematic versions.

- *The Scarlet Letter* by Nathaniel Hawthorne (novel, 1850)

  This is a popular canonical work that is accessible to readers at many levels and yet can be approached from many theoretical angles and provides rich thematic stimuli. Because it is a classic, the story is available in other media such as various film editions.

- *I, Tituba: Black Witch of Salem* by Maryse Condé (novel, published in French in 1986 and translated into English in 1992)

  This novel provides an opportunity to work with text in translation. This work is written from the perspective of Tituba, who was the only African-American slave named and tried during the Salem witch trials. It imagines her birth and coming-of-age in the Caribbean and subsequent enslavement and life in Puritan New England. The novel contains a pivotal inter-textual scene in which Tituba and Hester Prynne (of *The Scarlet Letter*) find themselves imprisoned in the same cell, albeit accused of different crimes. They develop a quick friendship and the scenes provide them with the opportunity to discuss the different realities experienced by men and women in their societies. Maryse Condé is a preeminent scholar from Guadeloupe in the French West Indies and is the author of many works of fiction and academic scholarship.

- *In the Blood* by Suzan-Lori Parks (play, first produced in 1999 and published in 2000)

  This play, set in the late 20th century, is a reimagination of *The Scarlet Letter* from the perspective of Hester, "La Negrita," an African-American homeless single mother of five who practices the letter A over and over in an effort to learn to read. The plays of Suzan-Lori Parks are distinctive for their avant garde forms and in 2002 won her the Pulitzer Prize.

This lesson highlights intertextuality and is itself recursive since the same story is revisited across differing temporal, geographic, cultural, and linguistic boundaries. Students often become trapped in the familiar terrain of character and plot analysis and find it difficult to move deeper into questions of genre, form, or representation. Presenting these texts as variations on a theme allows students to grapple with ever-deepening levels of literary analysis because the underlying story and the basic characters are already familiar. Experiencing how an original text can inspire the writing of others emphasizes a basic tenet of research—that knowledge is not produced in a vacuum, but is dependent upon its predecessors.

LEARNING ACTIVITY 1: PRE-READING

Preparing to Read

Before actually reading the primary texts, have students do research on the authors, the context, reviews, or theoretical approaches that may inform reading (Handout 9.1). Ask the students: "What might interest you about this text?" Doing these pre-reading exercises as a group will emphasize that reading is a socially constructed activity and will reinforce technology skills. Students often do not realize that they need information at this stage too, not just when gathering data to substantiate their arguments.

Creating a Database

Gather the results of the pre-reading research in a cumulative database, either on index cards or in a binder. If the technology is available, this activity can also be done by posting on an electronic discussion forum. The class can then refer to this knowledge database as they read the primary texts. As questions about the primary texts are clarified, contributions can be added to supplement the original research. I have found it helpful to require that students reply to the comments of others within a week after the original entries are entered in the knowledge database. This gives everyone a chance to read the contributions. This group activity prepares the class for an open discussion of the primary texts. Creating a reading community breaks the ice and lays the groundwork for doing the difficult work of close critical reading.

Pre-reading Research Methods

Use the following guidelines when structuring this learning activity.

Stage 1. Students may begin searching for information using informal Internet sources such as Google, Wikipedia, or Amazon.com.

Stage 2. Students will validate the information obtained from informal Internet sources using online academic sources such as *The Columbia Encyclopedia*, *The New Dictionary of Cultural Literacy*, or *The Cambridge History of English and American Literature*, all available at Bartleby.com.

Stage 3. Students will document all sources—formal and informal—as they collect data to prevent plagiarism and to develop the habit of compiling complete citations. Use MLA formatting for citing literature sources. Make students aware that bibliographic programs such as Note Bene are available and used by writers and scholars.

General Internet searches are a good place to begin this type of research and provide an opportunity to discuss note-taking, reliability of sources, summarizing, and search engine skills. A tutorial on using online databases or a trip to the library may also be worked into this activity. An online discussion forum is ideal for managing knowledge, but a communal box of index cards or a notebook would provide viable low-tech options. Even in a classroom with just one computer, the instructor can open a Moodle account and create an online discussion forum that students can use to serve as a knowledge database.

LEARNING ACTIVITY 2: CLOSE READING

Students who have little exposure to research or who have trouble concentrating may benefit from being led through each step of the cycle of writing in class, including doing the reading. Students may read a passage quietly for a few minutes to experience communally the introspection and silence that close reading requires. The over-stimulation of modern life, urban living, or busy households makes it difficult for many to find quiet time and it is important that students learn what that feels like.

Group reading will provide experiential knowledge of the concentration that reading demands. While reading, students can make notes, writing down unfamiliar words and concepts and anything they do not understand in the text. After setting aside time for quietly reading a short passage, the class can come together and share their lists and questions and conduct research to answer them together. This is an opportunity to demonstrate close reading and information gathering using various methods.

There are no wrong answers in reader reception. One interpretation is as valid as the next as long as each can be substantiated by the text. Literature is not like a mathematical formula for which there is only one right answer. In addition, there are nearly infinite ways of approaching a text.

As you introduce the topic of close reading to your class, distribute Handout 9.2.

Reading Research Methods

Students may look up unfamiliar words using bound or online dictionaries. They may need to look up biographical information or unfamiliar contexts using biographies and encyclopedias, also available online. Because the Internet provides instant and wide-ranging information at one's fingertips, having Internet access in a classroom is what makes this activity effective and provides an important opportunity for the instructor to model holistic research methods.

Conducting holistic research while reading also provides the instructor an opportunity to build in specific content. For example, as students ask questions, the instructor can access prepared lesson plans on the history of slavery, definitions of stereotype, or French Caribbean culture. Keeping a cache of these mini-lessons in an electronic medium, either stored on a CD, thumb drive, or in e-mail, takes advantage of the flexibility that technology provides.

Knowledge Management

After students clarify concepts, answer questions, and define terms, they can gather their collective knowledge in a database on index cards, in a class binder, or by electronic means on a disk, CD, or an online discussion forum.

As they continue reading, they can access any of this information and enrich their reading experience. Repeating the cycle of reading, research, sharing, and rereading slows down the reading process and reinforces the message that reading is a creative activity that calls for concentration, attentiveness to detail, and access to dictionaries and other information reserves. Some students will never gain experiential knowledge of this type of reading anywhere else, so it's important to take them by the hand and lead them through the experience in class.

Students then read a secondary text on feminism or have an in-class or online discussion of feminism. A close reading of the scene in question would be the ideal place to begin this discussion. Distribute Handout 9.3. Have students go through Part I of the assignment on feminism, then participate in Part II of the exercise.

LEARNING ACTIVITY 3: INVENTION

Rather than being handed a question or topic by the teacher, holistic research encourages students to choose their own topic and invent their own thesis statements. While invention can be activated by exposure to a stimulus such as a text, it is an internal process. Students must conduct the query themselves, must be moved to questions and research motivated by their own interests.

When students, who have been trained that literary research is a specialized activity, say, "I don't know what to write about!" I answer: "What have other people written?" Students may be perplexed about how to choose a topic for many reasons as varied as holding their skills in low esteem, lack of familiarity with the research process, or having a fossilized idea of research itself. When asked to share an opinion about a topic that interests them, however, they may have plenty to say. Ideas are generated based on observation. Reading is the act of observation in literary research. Questions arise out of close and critical reading; the closer the reading, the deeper the questions. Something you have observed makes you ask a question of the text or about the text. Holistic literary research begins at that moment of inquiry.

For these reasons, it is important not to discourage students from reacting to texts emotionally. Their immediate and most authentic response to a text may be an emotional one. As Brent (1992) emphasizes, readers "must also learn not to attempt to expel emotional reactions from the process of judgment" (n.p.). Research has shown that emotion plays a vital role in reasoning (Damasio, 1995). If students are going to have original and impassioned responses to literature, they must be allowed to follow their interests in approaching texts. This personal engagement in the act of close reading will build the momentum that is required for doing research and writing successful papers. Their passion for a subject should sustain them through the arduous journey from idea to final draft. While invention is by necessity an internal process and because one cannot force someone to be interested in a topic, instructors are encouraged to create an environment that nurtures the inner researcher, the inner editor, and the inner scholar. Students who follow their interests within the parameters of the curriculum and the lesson transfer the self-confidence and independence to research and editing. They develop the inner editor more easily and become not just independent learners but strong researchers as well.

LEARNING ACTIVITY 4: THESIS

Students are not necessarily aware that they need information, largely because they are used to passively receiving research topics from their teachers. I cannot emphasize enough how important it is to the development of holistic research skills to allow students to invent their own theses. This does not need to violate the demands of the curriculum. Even within relatively narrow topics, students can be allowed to formulate their own topics based on what they find interesting about reading. As you discuss thesis topics in class, distribute Handout 9.4.

Students produce thesis statements in class all the time while speaking extemporaneously. It would be helpful if the instructor pointed those out as the class argued about a critical aspect of a specific text by a specific author. Recording these potential thesis statements on paper or electronically can help students become comfortable with identifying the special characteristics of thesis statements.

Prewriting Exercises

Have students brainstorm topics or potential thesis statements in pairs or in small groups using paper and pen or electronic technology. Group brainstorming yields greater possibilities. Conducting research at the prewriting stage clarifies thinking, stimulates ideas and the imagination, frames arguments, refines questions, provides contexts, and grounds ideas in reality, providing a contextual lay of the land for a text. Modeling the kinds of questions and prompts that promote critical thinking about a topic encourages students to think about how they formulate their own questions.

Once students have brainstormed ideas, have them develop a hypothesis (Handout 9.5).

Group Evaluation of Thesis Statement

Use the available technology to share thesis statements in class. This may involve dividing up students into groups and having them read thesis statements to each other. Paper copies of the thesis statements may be distributed. If the technology is available, the thesis statement may be projected on a screen for the entire class to view. Go through the process of editing thesis statements and let the students watch a few times. Then encourage participation by asking students to identify grammatical, typographic, and spelling errors, as well as other errors in form.

This exercise provides yet another opportunity to engage holistic research skills through searching dictionaries, thesauri, encyclopedias, or databases as the need arises. Gradually guide the editing exercises toward higher orders of editing such as style, flow, structure, or logical fallacies that may appear in the thesis statements. Note that it is crucial to develop an atmosphere of trust in the class for this activity to succeed. Modeling gentle objectivity will help students overcome any nervousness about group editing. Never humiliate students. Humiliation or other painful learning practices are counterproductive to the development of a healthy inner editor.

LEARNING ACTIVITY 5: FIRST DRAFT

The act of writing is revelatory, and developing skills takes time and repetition. Writing assignments are rewritten several times and are designed to help students develop an inner, objective editor. To slow down the research and writing process, I assign short responses to close readings first, then a week or so later a thesis statement, followed by a first paragraph in the third week, and then a first draft the following week. This pacing prevents students from writing their drafts the night before the deadline. Group editing guides students through the steps of research and editing that they may be tempted to skip over. As peers read the thesis statements, first paragraphs, or first drafts, they may raise questions that will require the student to go back and research another aspect of the topic that had not occurred to them. Allowing students to eventually take control of the group editing process in class provides holistic opportunities for students to internalize word processing and editing techniques, reinforce how to identify strong theses and arguments, and tackle the mystifying strategies of essay structure.

After students have written their first draft, have them revisit their thesis statement (Handout 9.6).

LEARNING ACTIVITY 6: RESEARCH SECONDARY SOURCES

Now that there is a workable draft and an identifiable thesis statement and a potential structure, it's time to approach secondary sources with a fresh outlook. Students can continue peer activities in pairs or trios to evaluate thesis statements, define terms, experiment with structure, identify logical fallacies, visit online databases, and use dictionaries and other resources to redefine terms accurately (Handout 9.7).

Bibliographies and Documentation

The Modern Language Association (MLA) is the formatting standard for literary research. There are many reference books that outline the details of the MLA format. It is important to explain that whichever MLA formatting source one chooses, it should be consulted each time, not only to confirm that one is adhering to the correct format but because occasionally the MLA makes changes to the format.

The lesson on MLA formatting is also a good time to discuss the evaluation and reliability of sources. While the Internet has brought the problem of reliability to the forefront, good researchers and journalists know that "there is no such thing as an unbiased source" (Brent, 1992, n.p.). The holistic researcher carries over this healthy skepticism to all sources and all media.

Because all human knowledge is not yet available electronically, it is important for students to learn to use the brick-and-mortar library and its tools. A trip to the library and an introduction to the librarian and the wonders of library science is an important step in one's education. Unlocking the mysteries of library call numbers can provide enriching research materials. I often tell students to find the call numbers that correspond to their topic and to sit in front of that shelf and peruse all the materials available there. How have others organized similar arguments? This exercise can often result in unexpected finds and can take one's research down exciting and unforeseen paths. It is also an efficient way of grasping the breadth of a topic, of being introduced to unknown scholars, and of constructing a sound bibliography. Research can educate the student about using the appropriate terminology for the field, about how a particular topic is organized, and about other conventions particular to that field. This library visit is also a good time to introduce students to bibliographies and their usefulness to research.

The MLA publishes an online database that is available through libraries. Depending on their interface, a typical MLA database search will produce results that look like this sample:

Parks's In the Blood By: Kolin, Philip C.; Explicator, 2006 Summer; 64 (4): 245–48. (journal article)

> **Notes:** Library owns the following dates for this title:
>
> PAPER: 40(Fall 1981)-CURRENT
>
> MICROFILM: 1(1942)-39(1981)
>
> PDF Full Text

In this case, the search yielded a journal article about the primary text *In the Blood*. This particular result offers a copy of the article in PDF format containing the full text. It is important for students to learn the advantages of the full text option increasingly made available through bibliographic databases. If they can access the library online databases remotely, they would be able to simply click on the PDF or HTML "full text" link and read the article, print it out, and greatly expedite their research process. Increasing numbers of secondary sources are available in full text format. A lesson plan on the MLA electronic database also provides an opportunity for learning how to conduct successful searches and how to invent subject terms that will yield the desired results. Students often complain that they found nothing on their topic on the databases. The reason is often that their search terms are too narrow. A more general search is a better place to begin. For example, searching the text or keyword fields for "in the blood" and "suzan lori parks" will yield greater results than using the title and author fields. There is plenty of information available on conducting online searches. Encourage students to seek out research librarians, the fairy godmothers of researchers.

Other online databases that are useful for literary research and are available through libraries include:

- Academic Search Premier

- Literature Online (for full text and articles)

- Wilson OmniFile Full Text, Mega Edition

- *Books in Print* and interlibrary loan

- The New York Public Library at www.nypl.org

- Encyclopedias and databases such as *Facts on File* (for general research)

- Oxford English Dictionary (for etymologies)

- LexisNexis Academic (for newspapers, periodicals, and current affairs)

LEARNING ACTIVITY 7: REVISION

Revision covers many tasks including editing, organization, proofreading, and formatting. Lessons designed around the revision stage can also tackle narrative structure, grammar, style, and punctuation. Revision is a complex stage that students often think they have completed by simply proofreading their document. One solution is to slow down the process by introducing holistic research exercises with peer editing at the revision stage of the cycle of writing.

By modeling editing in the classroom using a projector or similar technology, students can watch the instructor edit documents. Demonstrating line-by-line editing and proofreading can give students a realistic idea of how much time they will need to devote to the task of revision. Demystifying editing is one of the most important missions of teaching holistic research in the cycle of writing. Students often ask about keyboard functions and mouse commands when they watch me do line-by-line editing in class. The more they learn about word processing and editing technologies like objects, pictures, graphics, and drawing, the more confident they will be about technology and the more prepared they will be for the workforce and for creating their own professional-quality portfolios and research papers. Editing and proofreading are largely dependent upon training the eye to accurately see the text on the page. The eye is a creature of habit and using a ruler as a line-by-line guide will help slow down the movement of the eyes enough to really look at each and every word. Precision is more important than speed, but practice will increase speed.

One peer-editing exercise is to have students work in pairs and edit each other's drafts. If the technology is available, instruct students on how to annotate each other's texts using the Comment function in Word. To create a comment in Word, go to the menu bar, click on Insert, then Comment, and type inside the text bubble that appears (Figure 10).

Figure 10.
Commenting feature in Microsoft Word

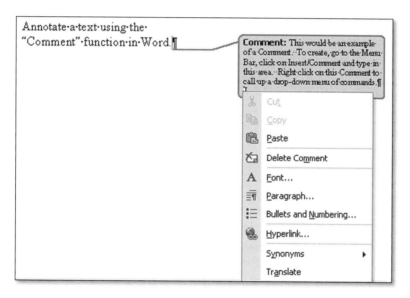

Peer-Editing Exercise: Committees on Editing

Based on errors that appear in their own essays, students are grouped into Committees on Editing (Handout 9.8). Each committee masters a specific category of grammatical rules, good writing practices, or research skills, and then enters its findings in the knowledge database, explaining the rules and how they apply. These groups of expert students offer peer advice. All students serve on committees on a rotating basis. Students can also present their Committees on Editing materials by doing short class presentations using PowerPoint or creating a paper manual demonstrating the rules they have learned.

LEARNING ACTIVITY 8: PUBLISH

Publishing the results of one's research is the final step in completing the cycle of writing, and it can take many forms. Portfolios, oral presentations, final conferences, chapbooks, anthologies, and performances all serve the purpose of sharing the completed project with others. This final step is often overlooked, partly because its importance is not appreciated. Undertaking a research project of any size requires a substantial commitment of time, energy, and psychological and emotional space. Sharing the culmination of all that hard work provides closure. Just as developing a dependable tennis or golf swing depends upon attention to its follow-through phase, sharing the results of a project and celebrating it with others prepares the energetic foundation for the impetus that will be required by the next project. Publishing one's work, like putting a period at the end of a sentence, provides us with a satisfying sense of completion that opens up an arena of possibilities for the next idea and creative activity.

Share Findings

The purpose of substantive writing is to expand on human knowledge. Critical thinkers communicate with each other and build on each other's findings. For this reason, others must be able to duplicate research results in order for the models proposed or conclusions drawn by the research paper to be considered viable.

Peer Presentations

The same balance of skills that defines good writing—the interesting, moving truth of the subject matter, the ability to work the audience, and the confident authorial voice—applies to effective oral and electronic presentations. Because public speaking skills are increasingly important and often overlooked, I offer guidance to students in developing their speaking skills in class. SCL offers students the opportunity to present their close readings and research to the class orally and through electronic means. Students may also be encouraged to present together and to incorporate multimedia tools that enrich oral presentations for both the speaker and audience. Allowing students to decide on their own presentations will also help them increase their holistic research and technology skills. They will practice changing technology genres: from print to video to Web to blog to wiki, to presentation slides, data-bases, spreadsheets, sound files, and anything else you'd like to try. Students get a chance to practice their PowerPoint presentation and video skills. Giving them free rein to create can yield creative results. For example, one student videotaped himself playing all the characters of a primary text and edited the video, added music, and presented it to the class. It was the most successful presentation of the semester.

Once students are encouraged to experiment with moving among genres and combining media in their presentations, they appear to be more engaged with the material and tend to produce interesting final projects that are both fun and reflect mastery over a greater range of skills.

Closing Events

Another way to "publish" research and complete the writing cycle is to have students plan a final event for the course. It could be a conference or panel discussions, or even a debate. Preparation for debates calls for many of the skills required in holistic research and their competitive structure seems to motivate students and foster team spirit.

Assessment

Distribute the following rubric and review it with the class after you have introduced the project, but before students begin substantive work on it.

Rubric for Technology and the Research Paper Unit

	Acceptable (Grade C)	High Order (Grade B)	Distinction (Grade A)	Relevant ISTE NETS·S	Relevant IRA/ NCTE Standards
Independent learning skills	Familiarity with and evidence of growth in self-direction in self-assessment, self-and peer-editing, weekly discussions, student Web pages, and other student-centered learning activities	Sustained self-direction in self-assessment, self-and peer-editing, weekly discussions, student Web pages, and other student-centered learning activities	Excellent self-direction in self-assessment, self- and peer-editing, weekly discussions, student Web pages, and other student-centered learning activities	1, 3, 4	1, 2, 3, 8, 9, 10, 11, 12,
Holistic research skills	Familiarity with and evidence of growth in research methods, including library online databases, citation to prevent plagiarism, secondary sources, technology literacy, information literacy, searches, hypertexts, and other holistic research skills	Sustained accurate facility with research methods, including library online databases, citation to prevent plagiarism, secondary sources, technology literacy, information literacy, searches, hypertexts, and other holistic research skills	Excellent fluency in use of research methods, including library online databases, citation to prevent plagiarism, secondary sources, technology literacy, information literacy, searches, hypertexts, and other holistic research skills	3, 4	1, 2, 3, 6, 7, 8
Presentation skills	Familiarity with and evidence of growth in methods of presentations, including software (e.g., PowerPoint) audio files, video files, Internet skills, oratory skills, clear, concise, logical, poised presentation	Sustained facility with methods of presentations, including software (e.g., PowerPoint) audio files, video files, Internet skills, oratory skills, clear, concise, logical, poised presentation	Excellent fluency in methods of presentations, including software (e.g., PowerPoint) audio files, video files, Internet skills, oratory skills, clear, concise, logical, poised presentation	2, 4	3, 4, 5, 6, 11

(Continued)

Rubric for Technology and the Research Paper Unit *(Continued)*

	Acceptable (Grade C)	High Order (Grade B)	Distinction (Grade A)	Relevant ISTE NETS•S	Relevant IRA/ NCTE Standards
Information and technology literacy	Familiarity with and evidence of growth in information and technology literacy including keyboard and mouse skills, e-mail, downloading and uploading, Internet browsers, finding, organizing, processing, and converting data	Sustained facility with methods of information and technology literacy including keyboard and mouse skills, e-mail and attachments, downloading and uploading, Internet browsers, finding, organizing, processing, and converting data	Excellent fluency in methods of information and technology literacy including keyboard and mouse skills, e-mail and attachments, downloading and uploading, Internet browsers, finding, organizing, processing, and converting data	3, 4	1, 2, 3, 6, 7, 8
Literary skills	Familiarity with and evidence of growth in literary skills including pre-reading, close reading, depth of comprehension, multiple drafts, editing, proofreading, document production, clarity of writing, logical structure, coherent argumentation, control of language appropriate to its purpose, primary and secondary sources, cohesive voice	Sustained facility with literary skills including pre-reading, close reading, depth of comprehension, multiple drafts, editing, proofreading, document production, clarity of writing, logical structure, coherent argumentation, control of language appropriate to its purpose, primary and secondary sources, risk-taking, cohesive voice, and style	Excellent mastery of literary skills including pre-reading, close reading, depth of comprehension, multiple drafts, editing, proofreading, document production, clarity of writing, logical structure, coherent argumentation, control of language appropriate to its purpose, primary and secondary sources, originality of the argument, risk-taking, invention of and execution of graceful style	2, 3, 4	1, 2, 3, 5, 9, 10, 11

Works Cited

American Library Association (ALA). (2006). *Information literacy competency standards for higher education.* Retrieved October 29, 2006, from www.ala.org/acrl/ilcomstan.html

Brent, D. (1992). *Reading as rhetorical invention: Knowledge, persuasion, and the teaching of research-based writing.* Retrieved November 12, 2006, from www.ucalgary.ca/~dabrent/rhetinv/rhetinv.html

Damasio, A. R. (1995). *Descartes' error: Emotion, reason, and the human brain.* New York: Harper Perennial.

Educational Testing Service (ETS). (2006). *ICT literacy assessment overview.* Retrieved October 30, 2006, from www.ets.orgportalsite/ets/menuitem. 1488512ecfd5b8849a77b13bc3921509/?vgnextoid= fde9af5e44df4010VgnVCM10000022f95190RCRD&vgnextchannel= cd7314ee98459010VgnVCM10000022f95190RCRD#seven

Eisenberg, M. B. (2003). *A Big6 skills overview. The Big6: Information literacy for the Information Age.* Retrieved October 29, 2006, from www.big6.com/showarticle.php?id=16

Howard, R. M. (2006, March 24). *Insufficient information anxiety: Rebuilding pedagogy for researched arguments.* Conference on College Composition and Communication. Retrieved April 28, 2006, from http://wrt-howard.syr.edu/Papers/CCCC2006.html

Jackman, L., & Weiner, S. (n.d.). National Forum on Information Literacy. Retrieved October 26, 2006, from www.infolit.org

Katz, I. R. (2005). *Beyond technical competence: Literacy in information and communication technology: An issue paper from ETS.* Retrieved October 29, 2006, from www.ets.org/Media/Tests/ICT_Literacy/pdf/ICT_Beyond_Technical_Competence.pdf

O'Neill, G., Moore, S., & McMullin, B. (2005). *Emerging issues in the practice of University Learning and Teaching.* All Ireland Society for Higher Education (AISHE). Retrieved April 25, 2005, from www.aishe.org/readings/2005-1/

Steyaert, J. (n.d.). *Information literacy star profile.* Retrieved October 27, 2006, from www.infolit.org/star_1.html

The University of Texas System Digital Library. (2004). *Texas information literacy tutorial (TILT).* Retrieved October 26, 2006, from http://tilt.lib.utsystem.edu/intro/misconceptions.htm

The Power of a Person Making a Point

Effective Public Speaking and Technology

STANDARDS

ISTE NETS for Students	2, 3, 4, 6
IRA/NCTE Standards	1, 4, 5, 6, 8, 11

KEYWORDS

public speaking, PowerPoint, reflective practice

OBJECTIVES

Students will:

* Critically reflect on appropriate techniques for a live presentation.

* Thoughtfully integrate media into an effective presentation.

* Create, rehearse, and revise a live presentation.

* Engage an audience in an informative presentation.

* Offer supportive feedback to peers on their presentations.

UNIT DESCRIPTION

Current technology now accompanies a medium older than antiquity—the live presentation. Not only is this medium old—imagine a caveman demonstrating the benefits of fire to his family and friends—but live presentations should continue to stay with us for as long as humans congregate.

PowerPoint has popularized the live presentation—giving courage to public-speaking phobics, in whose numbers I count myself. It has emboldened many to stand up and present, inform, and persuade a live audience. The problem is that as PowerPoint has raised the floor for presenters, it has also lowered the ceiling for the quality of the presentations (Norvig, 2001). In "The Plague of PowerPoint" Clifford Stoll (1999) describes an all too familiar situation.

> Today, the lecturer fiddles with a computer, focuses the projector, and adjusts his microphone. He pushes a few buttons and up pops a perfectly laid-out computer graphics display … you can include sound effects, cartoons, and clip art. But a hundred people have gathered to connect with a speaker, not to watch a light show. (pp. 180–181)

Often, the risk of stammering, getting excited, engaging with an audience is substituted with the safety of slide after slide of bullet points. Our use of PowerPoint exemplifies Thoreau's quip in *Walden* that "men have become the tools of their tools."

A moderator of a PowerPoint presentation usually violates some common-sense guidelines for engaging an audience. When a speaker moderates a slideshow, he is abdicating his responsibility to the audience. In the past, a presenter would surreptitiously look at his note cards because it was important to connect to the audience with eye contact. Not so with the PowerPoint moderator, who will unabashedly turn his back on his audience to read the slides, the same slides that everyone else is looking at. It is common for a PowerPoint moderator to distribute a handout of his slides. If you did not get the idea from the back of his head that he does not want to engage you, you will certainly get the idea when he has given you the option to skip ahead and generally ignore him. This experience is like asking a person out on a dinner date and then requesting separate tables and talking with cell phones. You have the audience there—use that presence and connection.

Besides boredom in the audience, PowerPoint can induce laziness in the presenter. The need to master your subject, memorize key points, and anticipate audience questions diminishes. Most of us create as we go, relying on the large size of our words projected behind us to buffer substantive scrutiny or questions—save for the obligatory second-to-last slide: "Questions?"

The worst part of this addiction is that it is being handed down to students. Like a mutating strain of a disease, the problem gets worse from one generation to another. The students make their presentations even more painful as they indiscriminately add flying letters and screeching slide transitions. The results can be intellectually vacuous content and a decision to put technology over people.

We must consider the medium, and the medium is not slide presentation software. The medium is a person in front of an audience—a person trying to inform or persuade other people in real time and in real space. The audience has been accustomed to appreciate eye contact, humor, logic, thoughtfulness, hospitality, and passion.

Yet public speaking that avoids technology does an equal disservice to our audience and our students. Images, diagrams, selected text writ large—original material and quotes from others—can be effectively used in the hands of a persuasive speaker. Blanket criticisms of PowerPoint run the risk of throwing out the baby with the bathwater.

This unit focuses on student presentations on independent reading projects, a component of the units on fanfiction (unit 2) and blogging (unit 3). This unit on live presentations can be applied to those activities or adapted for any time students are presenting in public.

The methods in this unit also strongly consider the vulnerable experience of giving a live presentation to peers. From developing the presentations to assessing the students, there are suggestions for developing a safe, supportive environment.

TECHNOLOGY

Presentation software, such as PowerPoint by Microsoft, Keynote by Apple, or Impress by Open Office (a free, open source program)

SUPPLEMENTARY RESOURCES

For a list of Web resources that is frequently revised and expanded, go to http://del.icio.us/cs272/powerpoint/.

The Cognitive Style of PowerPoint (Tufte, 2003)
    A persuasive booklet critiquing PowerPoint.

The Gettysburg PowerPoint Presentation: www.norvig.com/Gettysburg/
    Satirical example of Abraham Lincoln's speech with a PowerPoint presentation, by Peter Norvig, and a insightful accompanying essay (*PowerPoint, Shot with Its Own Bullets*).

The New Literacy: www.techlearning.com/showArticle.jhtml?articleID=47102021
    Interesting article on new literacy that argues students need to learn how to present information compellingly and match mediums and messages.

"The Plague of PowerPoint" (Stoll, 1999)
    Chapter railing against PowerPoint from *High-Tech Heretic: Reflections of a Computer Contrarian*.

PowerPoint Alternatives:
www.pctoday.com/editorial/article.asp?article=articles/2006/t0409/13t09/13t09.asp&guid
    This site offers an overview of software options for presentations.

ACTIVITIES

DAY 1

Students reflect on the medium of the live presentation that uses technology.

Start the unit with an introduction and a reflective activity. Before students start to create their presentations, give a general description of what the students will do—a live presentation using PowerPoint or a related media about their independent reading or creative writing source (or whatever topic they are presenting).

Ask them to do the guidelines activity (Handout 10.1). Many of your students will be familiar with PowerPoint from junior high or middle school. This activity is intended to help students reflect on the priorities and purpose of a live presentation that uses technology.

They do not have to agree with all of the guidelines, but it is important that they begin to think about the media and purposes of using presentation software. This is a method to scaffold them in developing their own values for a presentation. They should modify, disagree, or strongly agree with at least five of them. After the students have completed the activity, you should review each of the 10 guidelines as a class and get the students' feedback. Remind them that there is not a single correct answer, but also prompt them to explain or justify their answers.

DAYS 2–5

Distribute the presentation assignment (Handout 10.2). Students should be given class time to prepare the presentations. Depending on the technology available, students can work on computers or on paper, outlining their spoken words and images on the slides (Figure 11). You can print out blank slides with notes or have students print out their slides with space for the notes. This can be done in the print dialogue box. They can then work with you to effectively coordinate their slides and words. In practice, students can cut and convert these pages to note cards.

DAYS 6–7

Put your students in small groups to rehearse their presentations. Have students evaluate each other on the assignment description. If they know that you value rehearsal, they will come to value it as well.

DAYS 8–9

Give the students an opportunity to revise their presentations based on the feedback from the small group. Meet with them in small groups if necessary.

Figure 11. Outlining a presentation

DAYS 10–14

Have students give their presentations, and ask each student to fill out a feedback form (Handout 10.3) for each presentation. You will collect them and then share a "representative sample" for each student—I would recommend three to five comments. In this way you get to eliminate redundant or inappropriate comments and you give the students a manageable amount of feedback. You will have the flexibility to do this seamlessly if you describe this beforehand. I would strongly recommend focusing on the positive aspects of the presentation. Public speaking is an extremely frightening experience, and it is only improved with practice and a willingness to persevere. A student who makes mistakes but is encouraged to give more presentations is in an excellent position to become a good presenter.

Assessment

This rubric is different from the others in that it incorporates an awareness of the vulnerable position that teens put themselves in when they speak in front of their peers. It is overtly designed to provide feedback and not to audit performance. Distribute the rubric and review it with the class after you have introduced the project, but before students begin substantive work on it.

Rubric for Effective Public Speaking and Technology Unit

	Strength	Suggestion for Improvement Next Time	Relevant ISTE NETS•S	Relevant IRA/NCTE Standards
Used his or her own personal strengths to engage the audience				4, 6
Talked to the audience				4, 6
Interacted with the audience				4, 6, 11
Used media effectively			2, 3, 4, 6	4, 6, 8
Provided sufficient background information				
Provided appropriate handouts			2	4, 5
Kept the presentation interesting			2	4, 6
Participated in rehearsals and provided useful feedback			2, 4, 6	1, 4, 5, 11

Works Cited

Norvig, P. (2004). *PowerPoint: Shot with its own bullets*. Retrieved November 29, 2007, from http://norvig.com/lancet.html

Stoll, C. (1999). The plague of PowerPoint. In *High-tech heretic: Reflections of a computer contrarian* (pp. 179–184). New York: Anchor.

UNIT 11

iBard

Mastering Soliloquies through Performance and Audio Editing

Figure 12. ShakeStat, a statue of Shakespeare at Memorial, Oklahoma City, Oklahoma
(Image by BaronBrian, Creative Commons
Attribution License 2.0)

STANDARDS

ISTE NETS for Students	1, 2, 3, 4, 5, 6
IRA/NCTE Standards	1, 2, 3, 4, 6, 7, 8, 9, 11

KEYWORDS

audio technology, Shakespeare, poetry, performance-based approaches, Macbeth

OBJECTIVES

Students will:

- Interpret figurative language, dramatic techniques, and the poetic devices of a Shakespearean soliloquy.

- Build an understanding of a soliloquy in collaboration with peers.

- Collect appropriate resources from the Internet.

- Apply media, vocal, and technical strategies to interpret a text.

- Analyze the effects of various spoken techniques and digital effects.

- Apply legal and ethical principles of copyright and intellectual property in a productive and thoughtful way.

UNIT DESCRIPTION

When many students turn the page of a Shakespeare play and come to a soliloquy, they hit the invisible wall of reading—a frustratingly full page of uninterrupted text in dense and unfamiliar language, usually during an already challenging reading process. Understanding the soliloquies can be a turnkey experience for students in the comprehension of plot, character, and Shakespeare's language.

This activity uses audio technology to build on performance-based approaches to teach the soliloquies. Students begin by slowing down the language and exploring its meaning and nuance through selected dramatic and choral reading techniques and then enhance recordings of these dramatic readings with digital audio techniques. Many movies and some live performances enhance the dramatic effects of a soliloquy or speech with a voiceover or a disembodied voice. These spoken interpretations are further enhanced with music, sound effects, and audio techniques such as reverberation and echo. Film productions of Branagh's *Hamlet* and Polanski's *Macbeth* offer examples of these techniques. They can be done with soliloquies, long narrative poems, or dense prose. Enhancements can be done as an individual activity or used as part of a larger unit involving scene performances or soliloquy studies.

Performance-based approaches to working with soliloquies offer ways for students to slow down and internalize the language. They do this through techniques such as choral readings, alternating lines between two students, and increasing the volume of the speech. During these activities students are prompted to reflect on the internal arguments, rising emotions, and figurative language of the soliloquy. Using audio-editing technologies adds an extra dimension to this work.

Students create an audio recording of a soliloquy and then purposefully modify the recording of the voice with echo, reverberation, changes in pitch, amplification, fades, and a dozen other effects. They also mix in music and sound effects. Afterwards, they reflect and discuss their creative decisions and how these decisions contributed to the overall dramatic effect of the soliloquy.

TECHNOLOGY

computers with Internet access

Audacity audio-editing software

a microphone

downloaded MP3s

SUPPLEMENTARY RESOURCES

For lists of Web resources that are frequently revised and expanded, go to:
http://del.icio.us/cs272/ibard
http://del.icio.us/cs272/shakespeare
http://del.icio.us/cs272/audio

Resources for Teachers

Discovering Shakespeare's Language (Gibson & Field-Pickering, 1998)
Effective and innovative lessons for teaching a variety of topics, devices, and techniques of Shakespeare's language.

In Search of Shakespeare: www.pbs.org/shakespeare/educators/language/casestudy2.html
The Soliloquies Buster handout offers a variety of techniques for teaching soliloquies.

Macbeth, Cambridge School Shakespeare (Gibson, 2005)
>This edition comes with excellent performance-based ideas for teaching.

Shakespeare Set Free: Teaching Romeo and Juliet, Macbeth and A Midsummer Night's Dream (O'Brien, 1993)
>Excellent day-by-day lessons for teaching the plays through performance.

Resources for Teachers and Students

A Shakespeare Glossary, 3rd Ed. (Onions, 1986)
>Very good, concise reference for Shakespeare's words.

Macbeth: www-tech.mit.edu/Shakespeare/macbeth/
>Full text online.

Macbeth, Folger Shakespeare Library (edited by Barbara A. Mowat and Paul Werstine, 2004)
>Scene summaries and easy-to-use glosses make this a good student edition.

Online Shakespeare Glossary: www.onlineshakespeare.com/glossaryal.htm
>Good online reference of words from the plays.

Shakespeare Lexicon and Quotation Dictionary (Schmidt, 1971)
>Good reference, more comprehensive than Onions' work.

Film

Macbeth (Polanski, director, 1971)
>Good film version.

Macbeth (Welles, director, 1948)
>Another good film version.

Throne of Blood (Kurosawa, director, 1957)
>Japanese film adaptation of *Macbeth*.

Audio Resources for Music and Sound Effects

Audacity Tutorial: http://Web.njcu.edu/sites/faculty/cshamburg/Content/audacity.asp
>Short hands-on tutorial with accompanying sound files.

ccMixter: http://ccmixter.org

The Freesound Project: http://freesound.iua.upf.edu

FindSounds: www.findsounds.com

GarageBand: www.garageband.com

Magnatune: http://magnatune.com

For this unit, please refer to chapter 3 (on copyright) and appendix A (on using audio).

ACTIVITIES

Although the focus here is on *Macbeth*, this unit can be done before, in the middle of, or at the end of the study of any Shakespeare play. It can also be done as an independent unit on Shakespeare's soliloquies, using material from a variety of plays.

DAYS 1–2

Students are engaged in collaborative performances of soliloquies

Before you begin using the audio-editing technology, you should get the students on their feet and engage them in various dramatic and choral readings of the soliloquy. Have the students read Macbeth's soliloquy from Act 1, Scene 7 ("If it were done when 'tis done …") carefully for homework, marking any words or phrases that are unfamiliar to them. When class begins the next day, use a basic dictionary or Onions' *Shakespeare Glossary* to explicate unfamiliar words and phrases. The best way to do this is to go around the room and have each student read a line and then ask if there are any questions. Don't dwell on this for more than 10 minutes. Many of the phrases defy a single or simple interpretation and are best understood in the context of performance.

Because most soliloquies involve some inner conflict or internal debate in a character, getting students to read with various effects in two facing groups will go a long way toward exposing the meaning and effects of the speech.

Give the students Handouts 11.1 and 11.2. Each handout is a script that breaks up the text differently—the first one by lines and the second one by punctuation marks (with some slight deviations to preserve meaning). Having the students use both scripts will give them a sense of the dramatic and poetic nuances that blank verse provokes as well as illustrate that the meaning can get lost on novice readers because of enjambment and caesura.

As the students face off, instruct them to take turns and alternate down the two facing sides. Tell the first students to begin reading the lines in a whisper and then increase the volume so that the students at the end of the lines will be shouting (Figure 13).

Figure 13. Diagram of two student lines alternately raising the volume of a soliloquy

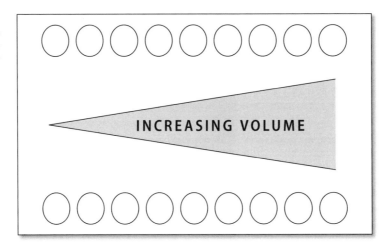

INCREASING VOLUME

Experiment with other vocal techniques, such as having:

- One side shout and the other side whisper

- One side whisper in unison and the other side take turns reading loudly

- The individual students take turns walking toward each other, meeting in the middle, saying the lines, and switching sides

Any other technique that has students reading, saying, and interpreting the words as a group will be extremely effective and engaging. You should do at least two different techniques so that students begin to understand the protean nature of the language and become familiar with saying it, in a safe environment. If you have an uneven number of students, you can participate or have another student double up. This is the foundation for close analysis of the text later.

DAYS 3–4

The teacher facilitates the audio production of one soliloquy.

For the next step you will introduce the students to the project of creating a group version of an iBard. You should create four groups. Three groups will work on the vocal aspects and one group will work on the sound effects. Dividing up labor into groups where each student is getting only a partial experience of the full project is generally not a good idea. However, this day's activity is designed to give the class a template of what every group and every student will be working on more extensively.

During this step you will create an iBard soliloquy of "Is this a dagger which I see before me" from Act 1, Scene 2 (Handout 11.3). If this is your first use of the digital audio-editing software Audacity, it is a relatively easy learning experience. Several tutorials are available—the Supplementary Resources section here and appendix A offer links to tutorials. You can scale your students' use of technology from minimal to extensive, depending on their prior use of the software, your time, your plans to use it further, and your knowledge of your students.

Distribute Handouts 11.3 and 11.4, and review the directions. You will record the groups on a single computer, one group at a time, using Audacity. After the first three groups have recorded their vocal interpretations (Figure 14), the fourth group will tell you where they want the sound effects and music (Figure 15). You should download the music beforehand to facilitate the editing of the project. *It is important to emphasize the broad licenses on the audio files listed on Handout 11.4.* If you have not covered the legal and ethical uses of media, this is a good opportunity to review fair use, copyright, and copyleft with a description of Creative Commons licenses and the specific licenses of the sound effects and music (see chapter 3). This might push this activity into another day, but it is worth the effort.

In these days of modeling, the teacher is the facilitator for the entire class's collaborative work. However, this is only done to give a simple and broad model of the procedures and technology of the iBard project. In the ensuing days, the students will take ownership of their own work. Again, depending on the length of your class period and any previous work with Audacity, this can take one to three class periods. This activity ends with the class listening to the entire collaborative endeavor.

Figure 14. Screenshot of vocal recordings of groups 1, 2, and 3

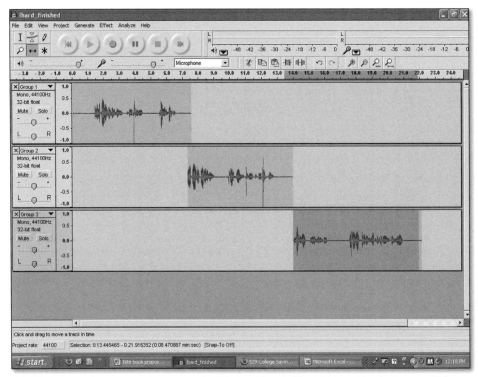

Audacity is a trademark of Dominic Mazzoni. Creative Commons 2.0 License

Figure 15. Screenshot of combined group vocals with two sound effects and music added

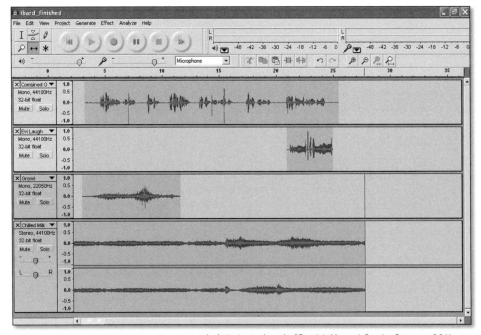

Audacity is a trademark of Dominic Mazzoni. Creative Commons 2.0 License

DAYS 5–10

Students work in groups to create their own audio versions of soliloquies. Students are given the reflective worksheet and the rubric.

You are now ready to have the students work on their own iBards. Give them the reflective worksheet (Handout 11.8) and the rubric, resources, and a time limit, and work with each group as they make their decisions.

It is suggested that you give the different groups the same soliloquy so they can see multiple interpretations of the same work, thereby increasing their understanding. The three soliloquies listed on Handouts 11.5, 11.6, and 11.7 would work well with six groups of four to five students.

This assignment is not to assess the technical expertise of the students, but to engage them in making thoughtful decisions on an interpretation of the text. In fact, there is no direct assessment of technical expertise. The software is relatively easy to use. This project and assessment focuses on the students' analytic and interpretive work on Shakespeare's text. Remember, you should distribute the reflective worksheet (Handout 11.8) before the students begin their group project.

Assessment

This rubric should be distributed after students are given their group projects (around Day 5). Two items on this rubric stand out as exemplars of the expression "assess what you value and others will value what you assess." The item for "Audio effects" emphasizes the judicious use of music; a temptation for students is to go overboard with these effects. Students will value restraint here because they are being reminded and assessed on it. Also, the item "Use of other media" emphasizes citing other media and works well with the use of Creative Commons materials. Students will more likely value the ethical use of other people's work because it is overtly assessed in the rubric.

Rubric for Mastering Soliloquies through Performance and Audio Editing

	Approaches	Meets	Exceeds	Relevant ISTE NETS•S	Relevant IRA/ NCTE Standards
Vocal techniques	Little or no connection between vocal techniques and interpretation of text in recording and worksheet	Some connection between vocal techniques and interpretation of text implied in recording and worksheet	Clear connection between vocal techniques and interpretation of text in recording and worksheet	1, 2, 4	1, 2, 3, 4, 6, 9, 12
Sound effects	Little or no connection among choice of effect, placement of effect, and interpretation of text in recording and worksheet	Some connection among choice of effect, placement of effect, and interpretation of text in recording and worksheet	Clear connection among choice of effect, placement of effect, and interpretation of text in recording and worksheet	1, 2, 4	3, 6, 7, 8
Music	Little or no connection among choice of song, placement of song, and interpretation of text in recording and worksheet	Some connection among choice of song, placement of song, and interpretation of text in recording and worksheet	Clear connection among choice of song, placement of song, and interpretation of text in recording and worksheet	1, 2, 4	1, 3, 7, 6, 8, 11, 12
Audio effects (echo, reverberation, etc.)	Random or excessive use of audio effects	Appropriate use of audio effects, yet some excessive traits	Appropriate and judicious use of audio effects	1, 2, 4, 6	1, 3, 6, 7, 8, 11, 12
Use of other media	Poor or no citations of media OR irresponsible use of other people's creative works	Some citations of media AND responsible use of other people's creative works	Full citations of all media AND responsible use of other people's creative works	1, 2, 3, 5, 6	7, 8

UNIT 12

Hamlet's Ghosts
Teaching Shakespeare with Film and Images

STANDARDS

ISTE NETS for Students	1, 2, 3, 4, 6
IRA/NCTE Standards	1, 2, 3, 4, 5, 7, 8, 9, 11

KEYWORDS

media techniques, Hamlet, viewing, video, digital storytelling, digital images

OBJECTIVES

Students will:

- Edit scenes from a play and convey both the poetry and the events of the scene.

- Analyze different videos of a scene and produce consistent evidence of close and careful viewing.

- Create digital stories with original and researched images that embody the action of the scene.

- Create a hypertext with accurate, thoughtful, and well-referenced links.

UNIT DESCRIPTION

Shakespeare's plays are wonderful to teach not just for their beautiful language and insights into human nature, but also because of the variety of interpretations they are open to. This is a boon as it fits well with student-centered approaches to teaching and the exploration of multiple perspectives.

However, many students have trouble allowing for ambiguity. One particular difficulty when teaching students a book or play that has been made into a movie is the students' adamant preconceptions of the story based on a particular movie version. For example, in the late 1990s many students fell in love with Baz Luhrmann's *Romeo + Juliet*. The enthusiasm is gratifying, but it comes with a price—students with a rigid idea about the play. This is particularly a problem with Shakespeare, in which the multiple interpretations and ambiguities of the text can be rich teaching opportunities. The plays are open to a variety of "right" interpretations for staging, acting, and set design.

Figure 16. David
Pascoe as the Ghost
in a University of
Rochester production
of *Hamlet*

Reprinted with permission of University of Rochester.

This unit uses movies, digital images, digital storytelling, and hypertext to help students explore the ambiguities and interpretations of a scene in a Shakespeare play. The activities focus on *Hamlet*, but the techniques can be applied to other Shakespeare plays or non-Shakespearean works.

This unit offers a template that begins by getting students to critically analyze multiple cinematic interpretations. They then capitalize on this experience and create their own version of the play using digital storytelling technologies, digital photography, and digital images of paintings of the scenes.

Students work in four interrelated mediums with a focus on varied interpretations:

- Text

- Cinematic productions of the works

- Digital storytelling

- Hypertext

These approaches can be applied separately and on different scenes in different plays. This unit will use as a model Act 1, Scenes 4 and 5, of *Hamlet*—when Hamlet first sees the ghost of his father.

Figure 17. From Boydell's Shakespeare Prints; illustration in Boydell is based on the original painting of 1789 by Fuseli

TECHNOLOGY

VCR or DVD player

digital storytelling software (see appendix B)

GarageBand (Apple)

iPhoto (Apple)

Photo Story (Microsoft)

HTML editor (Adobe Dreamweaver, Microsoft Word or FrontPage, Netscape Composer)

digital photography (optional)

Internet

Wikis

SUPPLEMENTARY RESOURCES

For lists of Web resources that are frequently revised and expanded, go to http://del.icio.us/cs272/shakespeare/ and http://del.icio.us/cs272/video/.

Selected Video Versions

Hamlet (Olivier, director)
The 1948 version written by, directed by, and starring Laurence Olivier.

Hamlet (Richardson, director)
The 1969 version starring Nicole Williamson.

Hamlet (Zeffirelli, director)
> The 1990 version starring Mel Gibson.

Hamlet (Branagh, director)
> The 1996 version starring and directed by Kenneth Branagh.

Hamlet (Almereyda, director)
> The 2000 version starring Ethan Hawke.

Books by Marvin Rosenberg

Marvin Rosenberg's books detail the performance history of several plays, interesting grist for teaching and performance.

Masks of Hamlet

Masks of Othello

Masks of King Lear

Masks of Anthony and Cleopatra

Videos about Hamlet

Discovering Hamlet
> Documentary that captures the production of Kenneth Branagh's stage production.

The Great Hamlets (Parts I and II)
> Documentary that examines scenes and characters from *Hamlet* with interviews from international actors on their interpretations and analysis.

The Independent Film Channel's Film School: www3.ifctv.com/filmschool/teachers.php
> Lesson plans and a glossary of film techniques with video examples from young filmmakers. The glossary of shots has numerous terms, but you can create a basic film vocabulary of terms such as *panning, arc shot, dissolve reaction shot,* and *soft focus.*

Digital Images of Hamlet

Hamlet on the Ramparts: http://shea.mit.edu/ramparts/collections/art/

ACTIVITIES

DAYS 1–2

Students take ownership of the words by editing the scene.

This first activity primes the students for a careful examination of the scene. Distribute Handout 12.1. Read through the entire scene with the class. I would recommend going around the room and having each student read a character's lines. This will give you 32 opportunities for student participation, so every kid gets a piece of Shakespeare. In groups of four, have them cut the scene to 20–30 lines then to 10–15 lines. With four characters in the scene, they can take roles and read through the lines. If you have time, you can have the groups perform their scenes. Regardless, each group should read their final version, and you can discuss the similarities and differences in their editions.

DAYS 3–4

After students have edited the scene, they will be more invested viewers and more attuned to the divergent film versions.

Students participate in a group analysis of different cinematic versions of the scene. This idea is adapted from Mike LoMonico's 2000 NCTE presentation "Teaching Shakespeare in the Digital Age."

They view different cinematic versions that have edited the scene as they did, as well as see a variety of film and dramatic techniques. Distribute Handout 12.2 to groups of four. Have students watch three film versions of the scene, on videotape or DVD. I would recommend Branagh's *Hamlet*, starring Kenneth Branagh (1996); Zeffirelli's *Hamlet*, starring Mel Gibson (1990); and Richardson's *Hamlet*, starring Nicole Williamson (1969). These versions offer starkly different interpretations of the scene and the Ghost—powerful and frightening in military armor, soft spoken and humble, and unseen and heard as a disembodied voice (the voice of Hamlet himself). After students view all three scenes and answer the questions on Handout 12.2, the teacher can discuss the collective analysis of each version and compare the different emotional and artistic effects.

DAYS 5–8

In performance-based activities, textual analysis is embedded in students' decision-making processes.

Students will create short digital videos using excerpts from the scene. With digital story-telling software such as GarageBand, iPhoto, or Photo Story, students can create montages of images—images of them enacting the scene interspersed with images of paintings of the scenes.

Distribute Handout 12.3 and keep the students in the groups of four. Students take still pictures of themselves enacting the scene and incorporate outside images (e.g., paintings of the scene, images of establishing shots, images of ghosts and castles). Students can do a Web search for images or go to Hamlet on the Ramparts (http://shea.mit.edu/ramparts/collections/art/), which stocks more than 100 digital images of famous paintings of this particular scene. They then add the dialogue to the digital story (from Handout 12.3) as well as sound effects and music (for sources see chapter 3, appendix A, and unit 11).

Before you begin, review terms such as *panning, dissolve, establishing shot, reaction shot, fade, close-up, cut, zoom,* and *fade.* The Independent Film Channel (www3.ifctv.com/filmschool/teachers.php) has a glossary for students and teachers, and many of the terms come with video examples. Students can use Handout 12.4 to help them organize their material.

DAYS 9–12

Hypertexting a passage gets students to slow down the language.

The prefix "hyper" refers to both the type of text and the more general state of being extremely active—both senses are appropriate for this activity of hypertexting. For this activity students must choose 8–10 lines of the text from the scene and add 8–10 hyperlinks or footnotes. These should include possible stage directions, definitions, interpretations of meanings, literary devices, and (for advanced students) textual variants. The goal is to provide a deep understanding of the text. This can be done with hypertext or you can expand on it with a wiki. You can do the hypertext with a variety of HTML editing programs (Netscape Composer, Dreamweaver, FrontPage) or Microsoft Word. You can also use the commenting or footnoting features of Word for different effects. Figure 18 is an example of the content of a hypertexted passage.

Figure 18. Model of hypertexted Hamlet passage

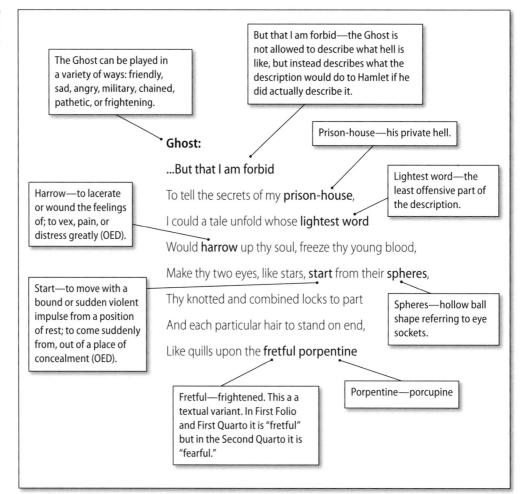

Assessment

This is a single, simple rubric for each of the parts of the project. You should review and discuss each rubric item after introducing each of the four tasks of the project.

Rubric for Teaching Shakespeare with Film and Images

	Approaches	Meets	Exceeds	Relevant ISTE NETS•S	Relevant IRA/ NCTE Standards
Textual edits	Edition does not convey the poetry of the language and the events of the scene	Edition generally conveys both the poetry of the language and the events of the scene	Edition effectively conveys both the poetry of the language and the events of the scene	1, 2	1, 2, 3, 6, 9, 11
Group analysis	Little or no evidence of close and careful viewing and thoughtful comments	General evidence of close and careful viewing and thoughtful comments	Consistent evidence of close and careful viewing and thoughtful comments	1, 2, 3, 4	1, 2, 3, 6, 8, 9, 11
Digital storytelling	Little or no integration of original and researched images and audio with Shakespeare's language	Integration of original and researched images and audio with Shakespeare's language	Effective and creative integration of original and researched images and audio with Shakespeare's language	1, 2, 3, 4, 5, 6	1, 2, 3, 4, 6, 7, 8, 9, 11
Hypertexting	Links are seldom varied, thoughtful, or well referenced	Links are generally varied, thoughtful, and well referenced	Links are quite varied, accurate, thoughtful, and well referenced	1, 2, 3, 4, 5, 6	1, 2, 3, 5, 6, 7, 9, 10

Work Cited

LoMonico, M. (2000, March). *Teaching Shakespeare in the Digital Age*. Workshop held at the National Council of Teachers of English Conference, New York.

APPENDIX **A**

Using Audio

IT WAS THE ROMANTIC POETS who trumpeted the aural power of language, extolling its ability to physically get into the body through the ear. Anyone who has seen the creation of sound effects or listened to an audio play knows the seemingly magical powers and creative possibilities of words and sounds. Today, podcasting and satellite radio have reenergized the interest and importance of audio. Creating audio works has students deeply engaged in a variety of language arts skills—researching, reading, writing, revising, speaking, rehearsing, and collaborating. They can also write and speak for real purposes and real audiences. The audio lessons in this book are feasible as well as engaging—the software is free; the technical instructions are easy; the equipment (a microphone) costs less than $10; and they can be done with one relatively inexpensive computer.

Many commercially available products for audio editing allow for multitrack recording on the computer. Multitrack recording is the ability to mix, edit, and control various sounds that are heard simultaneously and sequentially. Learning these programs is like learning word processing programs in the sense that 80% of the procedures and skills are common among them, and an understanding of one program transfers to another. If you can operate a tape recorder and a word processor, you can easily learn multitrack digital audio editing.

I strongly recommend Audacity, a free and open source program. It can be downloaded at http://audacity.sourceforge.net. It is a favorite of podcasters and digital audio enthusiasts because of its versatility and simplicity (and its price). David Murphy (2005) writes in *PC Magazine* that "the program mimics its more expensive brethren—Adobe Audition and Sound Forge—in providing recording and audio file-editing tools, and it's easy enough for beginners while including plenty of advanced features for audiophiles" (n.p.). The program is easy to learn and to teach. You can understand the fundamental procedures in a half an hour. It was developed through SourceForge (www.sourceforge.net), a collaborative Web site for developing and hosting open source projects. All you need is a computer and a microphone. If you do not have an Internet connection, you can download the program on another computer, save it on a CD, and then install it. There are both Windows and Mac versions. However, if you are a Mac user, you are most likely hooked on GarageBand, Apple's audio-editing and podcasting software.

Overview of Digital Audio

There are two types of recorded audio—digital and analog. Digital audio records and stores sounds in bits (off/on switches that are read by a computer). Analog recordings (audio cassettes, 8-track tapes, records) chemically and physically reproduce the audio in another format. The grooves on a record are an analogy to the sounds of the music—the music comes out when the needle translates the groves through the wires and speakers.

Digital audio is on your CDs, computer, and the Internet. Typically, a song or sound will come in a single file. The size of the file depends on both the length and quality of the sound. The ding you hear when you make a mistake on your computer is a small audio file—a short and simple sound. A high-quality recording of an opera is a large file. The most popular audio format is the MP3—it typically will have the .mp3 extension (e.g., ding.mp3 or laboheme.mp3). When making audio projects with your students, I recommend sticking with the MP3 format. This format is extremely faithful to the original sound, relatively small, and very flexible—it can be edited, transferred, and easily shared.

Streaming vs. Downloading

Knowing some basic digital audio terminology will give you a larger perspective of the technology. Let's start with *downloading* and *streaming*. Downloading is when an entire file from the Internet is copied from the remote location to your local computer. You will have the same file on your computer that was on the remote server. Streaming uses a different Internet protocol and a streaming server to transfer the audio and play it as it moves—drip by drip—to your computer. The streaming protocol has a higher priority on the Internet, so it is less likely to get interrupted or slowed. It is good for larger files and slower Internet connections. It also helps restrict the possession of the audio. For most practical purposes, a streamed audio file is an ephemeral experience, like a TV or radio broadcast.

Audio Formats

Besides MP3 there are other audio formats that you will come in contact with. The following chart offers a brief overview of the more popular ones.

Format	Comments
.wav	Common format in Windows operating system. Good for short sound effects and voice recordings. Files are relatively larger.
.ra, .ram, .rm	These are all Real Audio formats. They are proprietary formats developed by Real Networks and played with RealPlayer. Because these formats are typically intended for streaming and not for saving audio, it is technically difficult and possibly illegal to save and edit them.
.wma	This extension stands for Windows Media Audio, a proprietary file of Microsoft. It is often smaller than an MP3 because it uses the existing resources of the Windows operating system. However, it is can be difficult to edit and convert because of Microsoft's licensing restrictions.
.aac, .m4p	Apple's files for iTunes and iPods. Can be played on computers and iPods but can be difficult to edit and share because of Apple's licensing restrictions. Some of these files can be converted to MP3 files, but this is on a song-by-song basis depending on the restrictions placed on the individual file.

Sources of Audio

You can get audio from the Web, Internet services such as iTunes, or CDs, or you can make original sounds. Many people put audio files on the Web. To find them, you can access a basic search engine and use a song title and an extension, for example, "Oh Susannah" and .mp3, or you can use the advanced features of search engines such as Altavista (www.av.com) or All the Web (www.alltheWeb.com). Or, you can use search engines dedicated to audio such as Singing Fish (www.singingfish.com) or FindSounds (www.findsounds.com).

If you use a service such as Napster, iTunes, or Walmart Music, you need to test the transferability and editing of the audio. These services have digital rights management (DRM) applications associated with them. DRM is a way that content providers control the use and distribution of their material. For example, the DRM of a particular song may limit it to be used on one computer or only transferable to an iPod, but not to another audio player (see chapter 3 for more information).

One of the most difficult problems arises when students want to use songs, sounds, and samples on the Web. You are more likely to be covered by the fair use exception if you keep your digital editing in your classroom. An exciting and copyright safe resource is the growing body of work with Creative Commons (www.creativecommons.org) licenses. These licenses allow for a sliding scale of permissions from the creators of the work.

For example, the Freesound Project (http://freesound.iua.upf.edu) is an initiative that uses Creative Commons licenses as a fundamental part of its vision. The project's mission is:

> To create a huge collaborative database of audio snippets, samples, recordings, bleeps, ... released under the Creative Commons Sampling Plus License. The Freesound Project provides new and interesting ways of accessing these samples, allowing users to
>
> • browse the sounds in new ways using keywords, a "sounds-like" type of browsing and more

- upload and download sounds to and from the database, under the same creative commons license
- interact with fellow sound-artists! (n.p.)

Besides the Freesound Project, here are some other audio sites that employ Creative Commons licenses:

- Creative Commons Mixter: www.ccmixter.org
- Dance-Industries: www.dance-industries.com
- GarageBand: www.garageband.com
- Magnatune: www.magnatune.com
- OpSound: www.opsound.org

Creative Commons, copyleft, and the entire open source movement are exciting initiatives to explore with students when teaching the ethical and legal implications of using other people's work.

Ripping

Music and sound effects on an audio CD can be transferred from the CD to a computer. In the process the songs are converted from the CD playable version—the CDA file. Transferring from a CD to a computer and the necessary conversion to an MP3, AAC, or WMA format is call "ripping." There are many free programs (Windows Media Player, iTunes) that will do this for you. You can use ripped songs in your projects if you stay within the fair use guidelines (see chapter 3). Besides the options mentioned, you can also create original audio.

Other Resources

For lists of Web resources that are frequently revised and expanded, go to http://del.icio.us/cs272/audio/ and http://del.icio.us/cs272/copyleft/.

Audacity Resources

Chris Shamburg's Step-by-Step Audacity Tutorial:
http://Web.njcu.edu/faculty/cshamburg/Audacity.asp

Audacity Book: http://audacitybook.org/html/

Audacity Tutorials: http://audacity.sourceforge.net/help/tutorials/

Audio Resources Related to Copyleft

Creative Commons: www.creativecommons.org

Creative Commons Mixter: www.ccmixter.org

Dance-Industries: www.dance-industries.com

The Freesound Project: http://freesound.iua.upf.edu

GarageBand: www.garageband.com

Magnatune: www.magnatune.com

OpSound: www.opsound.org

Audio Search Engines

FindSounds: www.findsounds.com

Works Cited

The Freesound Project. (n.d.). *What is Freesound?* Retrieved August 1, 2006, from http://freesound.iua.upf.edu/whatIsFreesound.php

Murphy, D. (2005, April 5). Music utilities. *PC Magazine*. Retrieved August 1, 2006, from www.pcmag.com/article2/0,1895,1791624,00.asp

APPENDIX **B**

Using Video

TODAY'S TECHNOLOGY offers new, meaningful, and innovative ways to make students more advanced creators and consumers of video. The last five years has seen an explosion in desktop video editing. With inexpensive digital video cameras, video phones, and still cameras that capture video and audio, anyone with a few hundred dollars and a relatively new computer can create content that was previously in the realm of TV and movie producers. Students and teachers who have watched and been influenced by movies and TV shows can now actively participate in their production. The new meaning-making power has to be used in the language arts class.

Larry Cuban (1986) chronicles the history of film in the classroom in the 20th century—how film held the promise of being the tool that would bring the world into the classroom in the 1950s. The promise of film was not realized at the time, although the medium has been present in schools since then. The clunky 16-millimeter projectors were somewhat inflexible, and the slow move of VCRs and Betamaxes into schools in the 1980s did not lead to more innovative uses of films or video. Mike LoMonico (2003) points to a legacy of 16-millimeter projectors even in the age of videotapes: "The students would enter the classroom, the lights would go off, and the machine would begin to play" (n.p.). In many cases this was done after four or five days of studying the book as a reward for the students and the teacher, who might use the time to sit at a desk grading papers or tests in the darkness. The limited use of films is undoubtedly related to both the technology and the teacher-centered pedagogy that dominated the time. With a more learner-centered approach and the current pervasiveness of video and DVD, teachers have new options in their repertoires.

The units in this book focus on two complementary, learner-centered uses of video—students as viewers and students as creators. As the world's content becomes digital, the line between creator and consumer continues to blur.

Perhaps a reason that films and video were not used in more innovative ways was because they suffered from a respect problem. Films of books and plays were relegated to supporting roles, and the idea of teaching a film that was not previously read in class seemed like sacrilegious fluff. Movies matter; TV shows matter. However, they need to be taught for deep learning, not as a reward or a simple litmus test to capture students' superficial reactions.

Today, students can borrow movies and view them on their own or in groups; teachers and students can freeze and rewind scenes for discussion and analysis or study multiple versions of the same scene from different movies. The most important part of using films in meaningful ways is realizing that they are important. There are many reasons why film and video belong in the language arts class—the leading reason is the power the medium has on our psyches and our society. Also significant is the use of video as an accessible tool. Just as word processing was once the tool of specialist such as journalists, writers, and secretaries and has now become ubiquitous, video is now becoming a common application for communication. Joaquín Alvarado (2005) of the Technology Innovation and Employment Center in San Francisco relates how employers of architects, salesmen, and engineers are now looking for video-editing skills in their prospective employees.

Digital Storytelling

For creating video there are a variety of options—from editing still images and adding narration to professional-level productions. Digital storytelling is an exciting, practical technique with a rich potential in the English class. It is technically simple to learn and do in the classroom and generally involves organizing and editing images in montage with narration and music. Two popular software products can do this easily and well—Apple's GarageBand and Microsoft's Photo Story. GarageBand comes with new Macs in the iLife bundle, and Photo Story is available as a free download through the Microsoft Web site for anyone with Windows XP or higher. Both of these software packages allow you to organize, edit, and add a variety of effects to digital images and then export the timeline as a movie. You can add narration and audio tracks as well. You can also do digital storytelling with any video-editing software.

Other video-editing software gives you the ability to edit moving images—cut, add, arrange, and mix video with images and graphics. Though not as robust a technology, digital storytelling offers some pedagogical advantages over full video editing—ease of use, access, cost, and flexibility. I have created a hands-on tutorial for using Photo Story at http://Web.njcu.edu/sites/facutly/cshamburg/cshamburg/.

Video

Before you use a computer to edit and create a video, you will need to get the raw, unedited video to the computer. When moving video to a computer, you have to be aware of the two general types of video signals: digital and analog.

Digital sources can come from a CD, a computer, or a digital camera. The two most popular digital camera types are Mini DV and Digital 8. Mini DV works best with existing hardware and computers. It is what I would recommend to anyone interested in digital video. Digital sources are quite easy to transfer. Analog sources require some extra hardware—an analog converter—to convert the signal. Sources of analog signals are VCRs, camcorders, Hi-8, and Standard 8 cameras.

Digital video cameras, particularly the Mini DV, have come down in price and are convenient and easy to operate. You can get a good Mini DV camera for $300–500. Most Mini DV cameras will have two sets of functions—a camera and a player. You can record your video on a Mini DV tape and then play it back on your camera or TV. All Mini DV cameras come with an IEEE 1394 (a.k.a. FireWire) connection. Most new computers will have one. If yours does not, you can usually install it easily.

Once you have shot your video, you need to transfer it from the camera to the computer. You can do this only if you have a FireWire connection in your computer. If you do, simply attach the FireWire cable from your camera to your computer. Your computer and video-editing software will detect the connected camera and pop up a prompt to begin transferring the video.

Editing on Your Computer

Creating movies on a computer is often referred to as non-linear editing (NLE). Video-editing software is like word processing software to a novice—90% of the procedures are the same, so transferring skills from one program to another is relatively easy. Here is a list of some popular video-editing software packages.

- Final Cut Pro
- iMovie (comes with Macs)
- Movie Maker (comes with Windows XP)
- Pinnacle Studio
- Premier
- Premier Elements (a simple version of Premier)
- Showbiz
- Ulead Video Studio
- Vegas Movie Studio

For a comprehensive list of reviews of hundreds of video-editing software packages, go to *PC Magazine*'s video-editing review guide (www.pcmag.com/category2/0,1738,4835,00.asp).

Final Product

After you make the video, you can save it on your hard drive; burn it to on a CD or other portable device to transport to another computer; burn it to a CD in Video CD (VCD) format, which should work on another computer or most new DVD players; burn a DVD if you have a DVD burner; transfer it to a portable device such as an iPod; or put it on the Web on Google Videos or YouTube.

For a list of Web resources that is frequently revised and expanded, go to http://del.icio.us/cs272/video/

Works Cited

Alvarado, J. (2005). *Enabling education through collaborative digital media.* Retrieved December 1, 2006, from http://blogs.alti.asu.edu/2005/03/15/enabling-education-through-collaborative-digital-media/

Cuban, L. (1986). *Teachers and machines: The classroom use of technology since 1920.* New York: Teachers College Press.

LoMonico, M. (2003). Shakespeare on film. *In Search of Shakespeare* (PBS). Retrieved December 1, 2006, from www.pbs.org/shakespeare/educators/film/indepth.html

Resource Unit Handouts

Audio Essays

TITLE AND AUTHOR	Description from NPR	Link for Audio and Related Stories and Research	Link for Text Transcript
"Does Hair Make the Person?" *by Bianca Butler*	The relationship between hair and identity is a charged topic for some young black women. What does your hair say about you? What image do you want to project?	www.npr.org/templates/story/ story.php?storyId=5649817	www.youthradio.org/society/ npr060815_hairstories.shtml
"In Praise of a 'Girly' Muppet" *by Alix Black*	Facing competition from kids' programs like Dora the Explorer, the perennial Sesame Street has developed Abby Cadabby. She embraces her inner fairy princess, wings, wand, and all. Our commentator says it's nice to see a Muppet who's not afraid to be feminine.	www.npr.org/templates/story/ story.php?storyId=5641456	www.youthradio.org/society/ npr060812_fairyprincess.shtml
"The Effort to Keep an Online Diary Private" *by Bly Lauritano-Werner*	Bly Lauritano-Werner is a high school student with an online journal. Her mother reads the journal—but Bly thinks she shouldn't.	www.npr.org/templates/story/ story.php?storyId=5579002	www.youthradio.org/society/ npr060628_onlinejournal.shtml
"Kids Interpreting Medical Information to Parents" *by Anthony Jauregui*	In California, young people are often asked to interpret medical information for parents or relatives who are not fluent in English. But a state legislator believes interpreting sensitive medical information is too stressful for minors, and wants to ban the practice.	www.npr.org/templates/story/ story.php?storyId=5418069	www.youthradio.org/politics/ npr060509_interpreter.shtml
"Growing Up in a Coal Town: Stay Home or Leave?" *by Natasha Watts*	Commentator Natasha Watts is from the third generation of a coal mining family in Kentucky. The recent deaths of miners at the Sago Mine in West Virginia mirrored a similar mining accident in her home town decades ago, and reminds her of her own dilemma: whether to stay in the mountains with her family, or leave the coal industry behind.	www.npr.org/templates/story/ story.php?storyId=5147009	www.youthradio.org/society/ npr060110_coalcommunity_final. shtml

Audio Essay Questions for Study and Discussion

Each of these stories has a unique point of view and an opinion. Are there any elements or ideas that you strongly agree with? Disagree with? Are confused about?

What stories take an interest in media (Internet, TV, radio, or movies)? What are the authors' experiences and perspectives on the media they talk about?

What stories would you consider to be about political or social issues? Why? What does it mean to have a social or political theme in a story?

All of the radio essays connect a personal experience with bigger issues. Describe and analyze this connection in three of the radio essays. How do the speakers connect their personal experiences (e.g., an interest in a new Muppet) to larger issues (e.g., female roles, identities, and expectations)?

Four of the essays concern relationships between different generations ("Growing up in a Coal Town," "Keep an Online Diary Private," "Kids Interpreting Medical Information," and "Does Hair Make the Person?"). Describe the connections and conflicts between different generations in these essays. When do the interests of parents and children connect? When do they conflict? Do they ever conflict and connect at the same time?

What audio effects, quotes, interviews, and music did each of these essays use? How were they used and what effect did they have on you as a listener? Did these additions enhance or detract from the author's story?

Audio Essay Assignment

Pick an experience, observation, or interesting event from your life that can be connected to larger social or political issues. Write a 300–500 word essay on this topic. Share it with your classmates and your teacher for review and suggestions.

Think about the following:

- A recent event in your life
- An upcoming event in your life
- A current event
- A news story, recent movie, or TV show that is of personal interest to you
- An experience that you have gone through with your family or friends that might be of interest to others

How does your topic connect personal experience to larger issues in the world?

Record it and listen to it. How did it translate from a written piece to a spoken piece?

Could interviews, music, or other audio clips enhance your essay?

Be prepared to revise both the written and recorded versions based on feedback from your classmates and teacher.

Peer Responses to Audio Essays

You must listen to eight audio essays from your fellow students and comment on five of them. For the essays that you comment on you should address two of the following four questions.

1. Are there any elements or ideas that you strongly agree with? Disagree with? Are confused about? Please explain to the author.

2. Does this essay have an opinion on a political or social issue? Comment if you agree, disagree, or would modify the speaker's opinion.

3. Are the speaker's experiences similar to or different from yours? Please comment on the similarities or differences.

4. What one part of the audio essay did you like the most and what single part would you most like to change? Please describe both.

Analyzing News Stories

As you listen to the stories, focus your attention on the following characteristics:

- Does the reporter answer the five Ws (who, what, when, where, and why) and the one H (how)?

- Does the reporter use the inverted pyramid and begin with the major facts and then move into details and explanations? Do any of the stories circuitously state the main idea (use a buried lead)?

- How does the reporter give credibility to the story? Does he or she use interviews? Quote other people? Cite sources?

- Bias and balance: Do you detect any bias? Are legitimate points of view left out?

- Does the length of the story affect its quality? If so, how?

- Do different news sources have different styles or emphasize different aspects in stories on the same topic?

News Story Assignment

You are to write and record a news story on a school, local, regional, national or international event. The story must be 2–5 minutes long, and you need to answer the following questions in your final version. Submit answers to these questions with your audio file.

In the first 30 seconds do you answer the five Ws (who, what, when, where, and why) and the H (how)? Briefly list them or the reason why they are not included.

Who _____

What _____

When _____

Where _____

Why _____

How _____

Briefly describe the details and facts you supply to support your story. Note the sources of this information here and in your broadcast.

Are there conflicting points of view on this story? Did you include multiple perspectives? Why or why not?

How long is your story (in words and minutes)?

How would it change if you made it shorter?

How would it change if you made it longer?

Contract for Podcasting Unit

This agreement is in addition to the acceptable use policies and all other school policies. Failure to adhere to these rules will lead to an automatic grade of F.

Appropriate language. No profanity or obscenities in the most general sense of the terms will be allowed in any format in this unit—in projects or in communication with other students or the instructor. The judgment of profanity or obscenities is with the instructor.

Safety for self and others. You are not to mention personal identifying information about yourself or other people in any audio broadcast or accompanying document that is intended for use outside of this course—this includes last names, screen names, school name, home address, or any other unique information about yourself or others.

Respect for others. You should communicate with other students in the course with courtesy and respect. Disagreements are allowed, but must be communicated in respectful language. You must report any disrespectful, profane, or obscene language.

Respect for intellectual property. You may not use the intellectual property (audio, text, video, images, etc.) of another person without permission.

Adherence to classroom procedures. No work created for this course will be shared outside without the approval of the instructor. *All work will be submitted to the instructor and will then be made available to the public at the instructor's discretion.*

Any violation of this agreement will result in a grade of F for this unit. You also agree to report any known violations of this policy committed by others. Parents and legal guardians must also report any violations to the instructor.

_____

Student's Signature and Date

_____

Parent's or Guardian's Signature and Date

Source Material for Transformative Work

1. What is the name of the source material? _____

2. What is the medium of your source material? (circle one)

   Movie   Book   TV Show   Comic   Anime   Video Game
   Other:

3. Provide a brief overview of the original story and characters (the canon)—enough for someone with no background information to understand a story based on it.

4. Will you significantly change the events of the canon? Why or why not?

5. What characters will you include in your story? Briefly describe these characters as they are in the original material.

6. Will you significantly change these characters? Why or why not?

7. List any resources (books, Web sites, or videos) you think would be useful to understanding this topic.

Individual Reading Questionnaire

This is to get you thinking about your reading to date.

1. List the last three books you have read.

2. What has been the best book you have ever read?

3. Why did you like the book?

4. What three books have you not enjoyed?

5. Why didn't you like them?

6. Explain what makes reading a book easy or hard for you.

7. How do you choose a book?

8. What is the longest book you have read?

9. Who is your favourite author? Why?

10. Circle the types (genres) of book you like.

Fiction: Adventure, Romance, Mystery, War, Adolescent, Themes, Historical, Science Fiction, Humorous, Western, Fantasy, Horror, Suspense, Other

Nonfiction: Biographical, Autobiography, Sports, Encyclopedias, Books of Records, History, True Adventure

11. Do you visit or enjoy a local library? Why or why not?

Response to Individual Reading Questionnaire
(to be completed by teacher)

Texts and authors recommended for _____

This is an initial list of recommendations for your independent novel assignment. You can choose, use, or ignore books from this initial list. You will build on it in the next activity.

AUTHOR	TITLE

List Activity

Your task is to research lists in a variety of ways to produce a list of your favourite "top 10" books that you would like to read. Your teacher may give you a list generated from the recommendations of other students in the class. As well as this you can use Literature-Map to find new authors that you may like based on a favourite author of your own. Try it here at www.literature-map.com/.

When you have found some new authors, look them up at Amazon.com to read reviews of their books. Another way to research books is by going to Amazon.com and putting in a book that you have liked. See what customers who bought that book also bought. The following Web sites also have lists of books that may be enjoyable:

Ashland Public Schools: http://www.ashlandhs.org/ahs/pdfs/AHSSummerRead07.pdf

Books for Girls: http://amlib.eddept.wa.edu.au/Webquery.dll?v20=MarcList&v24=509178&v40=4422&v46=4426

Fresno County Public Library: www.fresnolibrary.org/teen/bn/authors.html

Houston Area Independent Schools Library Network (HAISLN) Recommended Reading Lists: www.haisln.org/ReadingLists.htm

What Should I Read Next?: www.whatshouldireadnext.com

YALit: www.yalit.com

Young Adult Library Services Association (YALSA): Literature and Language Arts: www.ala.org/ala/yalsa/booklistsawards/outstandingbooks/litlanguage.htm

Young Adult Library Services Association (YALSA): Quick Picks for Reluctant Young Adult Readers: www.ala.org/ala/yalsa/booklistsawards/quickpicks/quickpicksreluctant.htm

Questions

What kinds of books come up on the various lists?

What kinds of books would you like to see on your top 10 list? Make your own top 10 list.

Bring your top 10 list to class for discussion by the due date: _____

Blogging Rules and Etiquette

Blogging is a very public activity. Anything that gets posted on the Internet stays there. Deleting a post simply removes it from the blog it was posted to. Be sure that anything you write you are proud of. It can come back to haunt you if you don't.

Students using blogs are expected to treat blog spaces as classroom spaces. Speech that is inappropriate for class is not appropriate for our blog.

Freedom of speech comes with personal responsibility. Everything you post represents you. You shouldn't post anything you wouldn't be comfortable with anyone, from your parents or grandmother to teachers, viewing.

So, some rules:

- Avoid the use of chat language in blog posts. It may be OK in comments.

- Try to spell everything correctly.

- Do not post pictures of yourself. Remember to stay safe online.

- Do not plagiarize (copy things from someone else and pretend that you wrote it). Use hyperlinks to show where you got something that you want to quote.

- Make sure things you write about are factual. Don't post about things that aren't true.

When commenting:

- Treat all bloggers with respect.

- Seek first to understand what is being said.

- Celebrate another's accomplishments.

- Rephrase ideas in the blog that made you think, made you feel, or helped you learn. This lets the blogger know his or her voice has been heard.

- Comment specifically and positively, without criticism. If you disagree, comment appropriately, politely stating your perspective.

- Be mindful always that you may be a role model to your audience, especially if they are younger.

- Ask at least one question in your comments with the hope of continuing a conversation and deepening thinking.

(Adapted from www.langwitches.org/blog/?cat=2)

Blogging Activity

Now you have your blog. What should you do with it? After a time of reading your novel you should write a blog entry about your reading. You may write any questions you have about the novel, speculate about what will happen next, make connections between the novel and your own life, ask questions about what an incident in the novel may mean for future plot developments, and talk about what you like or don't like about the novel. You should have six blog entries before you return to school.

As well as this, regularly read the blogs of other members of your class. If you log in to your bloglines account, you can see when they have updated their blogs and you can read what they have written and leave a comment. You need to write at least two comments a week on others' blogs. Getting a conversation happening about the reading on the blogs is a way to get more out of your reading and is also an enjoyable activity.

Your last blog entry should contain a brief review (approximately 50–80 words) of your novel and a star rating out of five stars, with five stars being just about the best book you have ever read. Remember, your blog is public, and even the author of the novel you read may come across what you write.

Independent Novel Assignment

Choose one or more of the following activities to respond to the novel or novels you have chosen to read for your summer reading project. Be ready to share the artefact you create with the class on your return to school. You may want to publish your project on your blog or take pictures of it and post these on the blog.

Activities

Explain how you would make your book into a movie—who would play the main characters, where you would film it, and so forth. You must explain your choices.

Compare your book with several TV shows that are similar.

Make a video about part of the book and post it to YouTube.

Do a collage of newspaper articles or photographs and write an explanation of how it relates to your novel.

Do a piece of art about the novel. This could be sculpture or collage, pastel, or paint, or any medium you like.

Do a collage of a major theme of your novel or one that illustrates certain parts of your novel.

Find a movie that addresses a similar theme or subject and write a review (250 words) of it explaining why it is like your novel.

Make a scrapbook of pictures of the main characters. You could cut out pictures of people and animals that you think look like the characters and places in the novel, or you could collect magazine and newspaper articles.

Write several diary entries made by one of the major characters.

Pretend you are a character in the novel and describe the other characters in the novel and what you think of each of them. Explain why.

Interview one of the characters and then write out your interview. You might pretend that you are a writer for Who magazine. Make a podcast of the interview if you wish.

Write a newspaper story about what happened at the end or during a part of your novel. This will be a news story. Include a photo if you like.

Review the book that you read and compare it with a movie that is like the book. What happened in each? Which was better? Why?

Pretend that you're the author and describe the part that was the most fun or hardest to write. Explain why.

Write any kind of poem about your book. (Minimum 14 lines.)

Describe an experience you've had that was like the experience of a character in the book.

Explain why you would like to have one of the characters as a friend.

Explain how a character in the book changed from the beginning to the end.

Write a review of the novel to persuade someone else to read it.

What problems did the major characters have and how did they solve them?

Draw a map of where the story takes place and label all of the important places. On a separate sheet of paper, explain how the places were used in the novel.

Draw a colour map of where a major part of the story takes place. Label the major landmarks or points of interest. Use Gliffy at http://gliffy.com to draw the map or hand draw it.

Find a song or poem, or one of each, or several songs and poems that relate to the theme or subject of your novel. Copy the words or lyrics, and then explain how they relate to your novel. Or you could write songs or poems and then explain them.

Find three songs that relate to your novel. Copy the lyrics and then write an explanation of how they relate.

Write a long poem or rap (20 lines or more) about the book.

Use Microsoft Photo Story to make a presentation about your novel with your choice of music and images.

Oral Presentation Activity

Your task is to deliver a three-minute oral presentation about the book you read, focusing on the appealing aspects of the novel and presenting the information in such a way as to be useful for students who may want to choose that novel in the future. You are expected to integrate your artefact into the talk to the class. (Speak about what you did concerning the artefact or bring it to the class to show it.)

You will be assessed on awareness of purpose and audience; vocal techniques such as pace, voice projection, and appropriate use of palm cards; as well as duration of the talk and the integration into your talk of your independent novel assignment as appropriate.

Entries

Group 1

The Dunciad

The Restoration

Thomas Jefferson

The Age of Enlightenment

"A Modest Proposal"

Isaac Newton

"Annus Mirabilis"

The Wealth of Nations

Restoration Drama

Heroic Couplets

David Garrick

Aphra Behn

The Leviathan

Group 2

"A Tale of the Tub"

Satire

Samuel Butler

The Declaration of Independence

George Fox

"The Fable of the Bees"

Samuel Johnson

The Age of Reason

John Locke

Thomas Hobbes

An Essay on Man

Robert Boyle

The Tattler

A Vindication of the Rights of Woman

Group 3

Francis Bacon

The Diaries of Samuel Peyps

Quakers

Christopher Wren

Richard Steele

The Rake's Progress

Joseph Addison

Daniel Defoe

Alexander Pope

Jonathan Swift

Hobbesian

"Mac Flecknoe"

Mary Wollstonecraft

Group 4

Thomas Cromwell

The Glorious Revolution

John Dryden

The Mystics

The Beggar's Opera

Bernard Mandeville

Johnson's *Dictionary*

David Hume

The Great Fire of London

Adam Smith

William Hogarth

The Rights of Man

"The Shortest Way with the Dissenters"

Sources

Primary Sources

Primary sources are original materials. They are from the time period involved and have not been filtered through interpretation.

Diaries	Photographs
Interviews (including legal proceedings, personal, telephone, e-mail)	Proceedings of meetings, conferences, and symposia
Letters	Survey research (such as market surveys and public opinion polls)
Original documents (such as birth certificates or trial transcripts)	Works of literature
Patents	

Secondary Sources

Secondary sources are accounts written after the fact with the benefit of hindsight. They are interpretations and evaluations of primary sources. Secondary sources are not evidence, but rather the commentary on and discussion of evidence.

Biographies	Journal articles
Commentaries	Monographs
Dissertations	
Indexes, abstracts, bibliographies (used to locate primary and secondary sources)	

Tertiary Sources

Tertiary sources consist of information that is a distillation and collection of primary and secondary sources.

Almanacs

Encyclopedias

Fact books

(Material above from www.lib.umd.edu/guides/primary-sources.html.)

Textbooks are also tertiary sources.

Blogs, wikis, and podcasts can be primary, secondary, or tertiary sources, depending on their use. Please be prepared to explain your categorization. Wikipedia is generally considered a tertiary source.

Student Checklist

Wiki Entries

Create an 18th-century entry for your group.

Create a relevant modern connection entry.

Link to four other entries (these can be 18th-century entries or a combination of 18th-century and modern connection entries, depending on the instructions of your teacher).

Link these four entries back to your entries.

Edit four entries total (these can be the entries that you linked to or related entries).

Comment on four entries (other than your own) in the entire project.

Final Report

Write a report on your role in the entire process. Your report must include a description of your initial work—your 18th-century entry and your modern connection entry—as well as a description of the pages that you changed or commented on. You need to refer to pages by name and URL. You also need to include a history of what happened to your initial entries—who changed them, what they were changed to, and if you agree with these changes. You must also describe and respond to any comments that were added to your pages.

Brainstorming

1. Memoir title or topic:

How does this memoir begin?

What makes this interesting?

How does it end?

2. Memoir title or topic:

How does this memoir begin?

What makes this interesting?

How does it end?

3. Memoir title or topic:

How does this memoir begin?

What makes this interesting?

How does it end?

Terms for Editors

Begin all your editing with the following four terms:

Rephrase. A word, phrase, sentence, or paragraph is unclear or the editor has a suggestion to improve the writing.

Expand. An element of the writing is interesting or important and more is needed.

Move. An idea would work better at a different point in the text.

Delete. A word, detail, phrase, or sentence is unnecessary and should be eliminated.

For each term, the editor should provide a brief explanation. For example:

Rephrase. *This might sound better if you used a comparison—something like "he jumped up as if he sat on a needle."*

Expand. *This is a very interesting person. I'd like to know more about her.*

Move. *This description would be better early on.*

Delete. *You said this in the first paragraph.*

Script-writing Group

Begin by discussing basic elements of the story, and start to work on writing dialogue.

All characters should be included in your dialogue: the narrator; her husband, John; Jennie (John's sister); and the "woman" in the wallpaper.

Make sure that you include all the main events of the text in your script: the narrator seeing her room for the first time, her beginning to see the "woman," her husband's reaction to her emotional state, Jenny's reaction, and the narrator's "descent into madness," including her seeing the "creeping woman" and her "freeing" the woman from the wallpaper.

The script should be about 5–10 pages long.

You will have two class periods to meet and write, and whatever is not finished in class is to be completed for homework.

Make sure you also include directions for the camera crew in your script, such as when to cut the camera when a scene is completed.

On the third day, the teacher will review the script, and once it has been approved, will make copies for you to distribute to the actors.

During rehearsal and filming, it is vital that you be engaged, making changes when needed or giving input to directors and actors.

Be available for questions from directors, actors, the set group, and the camera crew. It is your script that is the fabric of this video. Work together and have fun!

Acting Group

Until you receive a finished script from the scriptwriters, discuss your characters and the important elements of the story.

Each of you should write a list of nouns, verbs, and adjectives for your character and then share this list with the other groups to develop a collaborative vision of the video.

Once you receive a completed script from the writers, do a read-through and begin preparation of the lines.

Memorization is not mandatory, but it is encouraged. If you do not memorize, make sure you prepare your lines so well that you do not have your face in the script during filming.

Any questions you have should be brought to the scriptwriters and directors, as well as the set and costume group and the camera group.

Look at your lists of nouns, verbs, and adjectives as you prepare your characters; these will help you to develop a fuller understanding of your characters.

The directors will begin working with you after they have reviewed the script, and you will then begin rehearsals.

You are all part of a cast, and should work together. You all can be very helpful to one another throughout the rehearsal and filming process.

Have fun!

Set and Costume Group

You are to discuss and plan the set, namely, the room with the wallpaper.

The entire video can be set in one room, because the majority of the action takes place in the narrator's room.

Once you receive the completed script, you can work from that, but until then, think of the basics.

You will design the yellow wallpaper itself, and draw the pattern on it. The teacher will supply you with materials, including markers, scissors, and bulletin board paper for the wallpaper.

Give a completed list to the teacher by the second day, and begin collecting your items. The costumes can come from your wardrobes, or you may use items from the costume department at school (with permission).

You do not have to create a time period through set and costumes. Pictures of period dress are available in books and online if you want to see them, but work together as a group to see what unique ideas you can come up with.

The actors themselves may have some items too; let the actors know what they will be wearing, so they can begin to look for their items. Compile a complete list of the props, costume pieces, and set elements you intend to use and give them to the teacher.

Work collaboratively and be sure to have everything ready prior to actual filming.

Have fun!

Directing Group

Get together and discuss the main elements of the story while waiting for the script. Once you receive the script, meet with the actors for a read-through. Any immediate questions should be directed to the script writers.

It is your responsibility to oversee the rehearsal and filming, but it is also crucial that you work collaboratively with the other groups.

You may use two to three class periods to rehearse, and then actual filming will begin.

You are encouraged to incorporate music throughout the video. You may use classical or modern music, and it is your responsibility to decide where to include the songs.

You may all work in a group and direct each scene in the video, or you may divide yourselves up and each direct a scene.

The camera crew will be working with you to figure out close-ups, camera angles, and other specifics.

In addition, the set and costume group will be providing input throughout, as well as creating the set.

Work together and have fun!

Camera Group

You are responsible for everything that has to do with the camera, including creating the opening and closing credits. These can be created on a roll of paper, which two of you hold up and scroll down for the camera, or by computer. If done by computer, they can be completed prior to filming, with the camera filming the computer screen.

Break up and move about the classroom, getting the names of everyone in the class, as well as their roles in the video. Make sure to include a title in these credits.

Once you receive a complete script, you are all to get together, read it as a group, and begin to discuss how the camera will be involved.

This is a video, and therefore the camera plays a huge part; however, it is what you all do with it that makes it the most interesting.

A camera crew does not simply stand back and let the camera do all the work. Work as a team, and remember, the more creative you get, the better and more exciting the finished product will be.

Have fun!

Liaison's Worksheet

Your name: _____

Your home group: _____

Group you visited: _____

Gathering Information

Did you discuss the project with each member of the group? Why or why not?

What decisions did they make to do their tasks?

How were these decisions supported by the text?

Giving Feedback

Share the above information with your home group, answer the following questions, and then share the answers with your liaison group.

What ideas were the most impressive to your group?

What idea was the most confusing to your group?

What are the main suggestions that you would make to the group you visited?

Gathering Evidence

Each pair is to go through the book and find the following information. You should quote directly from the book and write down the page number of the quote. For longer quotes feel free to use ellipses (…).

How does the narrator describe the character?

How does the character describe himself or herself?

How do other characters describe the character?

Preinterview: Actions and Decisions

What are the three biggest actions and decisions of the character? These could have happened before or during the time frame of the story.

1. _____

2. _____

3. _____

Interviewer Questions

Questions on Decision 1

Starter question _____

_____

Follow-up 1 _____

_____

Follow-up 2 _____

_____

Questions on Decision 2

Starter question _____

_____

Follow-up 1 _____

_____

Follow-up 2 _____

_____

Questions on Decision 3

Starter question _____

_____

Follow-up 1 _____

_____

Follow-up 2 _____

_____

Rules for Creating the Interview

Rule 1: Keep the facts. You cannot change the facts of the story. For example, Lennie cannot escape at the end; George is not secretly a millionaire.

Rule 2: Opinions are changeable. A character can dispute a characterization or opinion about himself or another character. For instance, Curley can dispute the characterization of being "mean"; Slim can defend Curley's wife and say that she is not a "tart."

Rule 3: Disputes on facts or opinions are welcome. A highly teachable and desirable debate arises when the line between fact and opinion is blurry. For example, Can Curley dispute being "a little guy"? Discuss these with the teacher, who will be the final judge.

Rule 4: You can add facts. You can add facts that do not violate Rule 1. For example, you can give Curley's wife a name or list books that Crooks reads.

Rule 5: You must add context. Characters can refer to specific historical events (e.g., the Great Depression) or social history (the status of women or the condition of race relations during the 1930s). There should be a minimum of two references to historical events or social history in your interview.

Phrases You Can Use to Start Your Answers

For Interviewers

Starter Questions

Why did you (important action or decision) …?

How do you (important action or decision) …?

Follow-Up Questions

But (another character) says you are …

So you say (another character is wrong) when (he or she) says …

Then why do many people think you are (narrator's description) …

For Characters

For All Character Answers

Remember when I said (description by self) …

Remember when I (narrative of actions) …

Remember when I was described as a (other character's description) …

I had reasons for saying that about myself …

Most people would call me (author's description) …

… Part of that is true, but it's more like …

… That's not true because I also …

… I was like that at one point but now I'm …

Listening Questions

Response to Listening

Name _____

Character _____

You have to address four statements in total.

What statements did the character say that you agree with? (List one to four.) Why?

What statements did the character say that you did not agree with? (List one to four.) Why not?

Brainstorming Topics

Name _____

List three different ideas for your video. Remember, your purpose is to influence or inform your representative or senator to act on a particular issue—one that is either well known or one that you want to make better known. Write down your idea and a brief explanation for why it is important for your representative or senator to know.

Idea 1

Teacher Feedback:

Idea 2

Teacher Feedback:

Idea 3

Teacher Feedback:

Resource List

Supporting Research and Quotes *(Use additional paper if necessary.)*

Fact, Idea, or Quote	Source

Effective Images

Image Name, Description	Source

Points for Narration

Points for Facts and Images	Related to Fact, Idea, Quote, and/or Image

Storyboard Outline

Organize the content and order of your material using the chart on the following page. For images, you can list ones that you have or will be getting. Your narration can apply to one image or go across several. You can also have images and video without narration. Please remember that this storyboard will be a starting point. You will change your content and organization as you develop your work on the computer.

Be aware that this video will be made public and sent to an elected official. Consider the effects of directly addressing a senator or representative in the narration or using a more objective tone.

Name _____ page _____ of _____ *(copy as needed)*

Audio Effect and Music:				
Images				
Narration				
Notes:				
Teacher Comments:				

Pre-reading Assigment

Before reading the primary texts:

Find the country of origin of the authors and the setting of the works. Go to the library's online databases and research some basic information on the authors and settings. Using these ideas to start research, not as limitations, find information on the following:

- Who are Nathaniel Hawthorne, Maryse Condé, and Suzan-Lori Parks?
- What are the books and play about?
- Describe the settings of the novels and play.
- For each work, compare the cultural context of the time of the writing versus the cultural context of the setting.
- What is the country of origin of the authors and playwright?
- What religions were present during the colonial period of the United States?
- Identify the distinctive constructions of race, gender, or class in each work, being careful to define terms precisely.
- Describe the history of Puritan society.
- Describe the history of African slavery.
- Provide any other information that might be relevant to reading the novels and play.

Make sure to paraphrase, quote, or summarize your findings and cite your sources accurately so that others can easily find the sources themselves.

Share your findings by the methods determined in class—index cards, gathered into a binder, or posted in an electronic discussion forum.

Once you have shared your own research, go to the research provided by others and respond. Make sure that your response supplements, expands upon, or provides counterexamples to the research of others.

Close Reading of *I, Tituba*

1. Taking the class discussion into consideration, read everyone else's research entry.

2. Look up a secondary source using the library's online databases.

3. Write an entry that reflects a deeper, more informed, closer reading of the same primary text.

4. Respond to the entry of one peer. Your response should either supplement or negate their original entry, using quotes from the primary text. Your response should reflect a closer, deeper re-reading of the text and should include the proper citation, including page numbers, when quoting.

Feminism

What is feminism? Part I

In *I, Tituba*, Hester talks about "feminism" with Tituba while they are imprisoned.

1. Write down what you think feminism is and save your description.

2. After you have shared your entry, read the entries of other students.

What is feminism? Part II

1. Go to any dictionary or encyclopedia and look up the definition of feminism.

2. Go back and read your original definition of feminism and note whether it has changed and if so, how it has changed. Write a 100-word definition of feminism based on the dictionary definition of feminism, our close reading of the passage, and our subsequent discussion. Discuss how and why your definition has changed. If you are quoting from a text, make sure to cite the source and the page number and to use quotation marks.

3. Once you have posted your new definition, respond to a peer's definition. Remember that your responses should supplement, document, or provide a counterexample of your peer's entry.

Create a Thesis Statement

In coming up with your own topic, ask yourself, "What do I find interesting?" That's the first and most important step. The other approach is to identify a theme or idea that was appealing to you from our class discussion; for example, race. It must be something that you are really interested in exploring. Once you have a topic, then you can create a thesis. It all depends on what *you* are interested in pursuing. Perhaps you come alive when reading the work of a particular author. The only important aspect of choosing a topic is finding something you are so passionate about that it will sustain you through the arduous process of writing a research paper.

Once you have a topic, ask yourself, "What is it that interests me about it?" After a few minutes of that line of questions, it is possible to end up with a list of possible research tracks; for example, race in the Caribbean, race and gender in *I, Tituba*, racial metaphors in *In the Blood*. Then go back to the text and figure out what you want to say about race, exactly. At this point it's helpful to go back to the knowledge database the class put together and look at the entries. They are full of potential paper topics that you can develop into a thesis statement.

Develop a Hypothesis

After having read the text and chosen a general topic, what exactly do you want to know? What is the question that you want to answer? Do research on your question. What have others written about your question? Formulate a hypothesis or a possible answer to the question the essay will attempt to answer. Propose a hypothesis based on your best educated guess about what the answer to your question might be.

Revisit the Thesis Statement

The first draft is just a way of finding out what we really think about something. Does your first paragraph state a thesis at all? There should be at least one but not more than one thesis stated in the first paragraph.

If the thesis statement is absent from the first paragraph or if it is weak, the genuine thesis statement can often be found in the last paragraph and sometimes is the last sentence of the first draft. Is there a competing thesis statement at the end of your first draft? If so, compare the two and examine their differences.

Does the body of your first draft eventually prove a different point than what is stated in the first paragraph? Chances are high that the arguments that appear in the last paragraph are clearer and more persuasive than the thesis in the first paragraph. This often happens because we use the first draft to tell ourselves what we really think about the topic. We are thinking on paper and this is the real purpose of the first draft.

Take the stronger thesis statement or argument that appears in the last paragraph, put it at the top of the second draft, and begin to reorganize the material so that it flows from this new thesis. Delete anything that does not support this new thesis.

Research Secondary Sources

Now that you have a workable first draft, consider:

What would other scholars think about this hypothesis? Are there other fields—psychology, sociology, anthropology, economics, history, literary criticism—that have tackled this same question? Test your theory by collecting data on it: Using logic and critical-thinking skills, evaluate whether the data, research, or the text itself substantiates your hypothesis or answer.

Doing more research at this stage would be helpful. Research provides data. Research provides information that improves decision making. This is also a good time to consult the research librarian. Persistence is the most important characteristic of a good researcher. Also important is the skill of sifting through general material to find that one source—that needle in the haystack—that will support your argument.

It is imperative that you document your sources as you do research. Do not wait until you have written your second draft. Keep careful records of full citations including page numbers.

Committees on Editing

Find my comments on essays I returned to you. Look at my comments carefully. Rather than correct your errors, I have marked each error by categorizing the error by type.

Everyone who has the same type of error will form a group. For example, everyone who has a "misused comma" error in their draft will automatically belong to the Committee on Commas.

Each group will look up all the grammatical errors in a style manual or other reference guide for tips on how to correct them.

Each committee will create an entry for each error. The entry should state the error, its correction, and the rule that applies.

The committees will post their entries into the knowledge database to share with the class.

Each student will then revise his or her paper using the Committees on Editing entries.

At any point in the editing process, students may consult and add to the knowledge database while revising. During the process of editing your papers, feel free to consult the other committees for expert advice on how to correct your particular category of error.

Guidelines Activity

This is an initial list of guidelines for giving an effective presentation that uses PowerPoint or other presentation software. Please make it your own by **modifying**, **removing**, or **strongly agreeing** with a total of at least five of the guidelines.

- Do not start off with a slide—start with yourself.
- Use slides judiciously. You are talking to the audience, not describing a PowerPoint presentation.
- Follow the principles of good public speaking and good teaching. Engage your audience in a variety of ways. Be yourself, be credible, and be knowledgeable about the topic.
- Give helpful and complementary handouts, not a copy of the slides.
- Do not read from the slides often.
- Avoid distracting effects (e.g., custom animation and fancy slide transitions).
- Consider the different effects on the audience of having varied or uniform layouts on your slides.
- Avoid clip art and use relevant images.
- Avoid too much text on a slide.
- Talk TO your audience not AT your audience.

Presentation Assignment

You will give a two to four minute presentation on the book, movie, TV show, or video game of your choice. You should enhance your presentation with some form of media—a slide presentation, video clip, or visual demonstration. The media should enhance your presentation, not be your presentation.

Your presentation should have the following components:

- **Use a presentation style that matches your personality and engages the audience.** You do not have to act like a game show host to engage your audience. However, you need to value the attention and interest of your audience. Enthusiasm and interest are contagious.

- **Speak to your audience.** Do not read from your slides often. Your audience can do that.

- **Interact with your audience.** You should stop at least two times during your presentation to engage the audience. Asking for a "show of hands" on a question or pausing after a specific point for questions keeps your audience tuned in to your presentation.

- **Use images, text, and media effectively.** There should be a compelling reason for using the media you choose.

- **Provide sufficient background knowledge.** You need to supply enough background knowledge to make the important parts of your presentation understandable. Many members of your audience might be totally unfamiliar with your subject. Before you convey the parts that interest you, they should have a foundation of understanding.

- **Provide handouts that are useful and do not distract from the presentation.** Please keep in mind that if your handouts duplicate your presentation, your audience members will be tempted to skip ahead or read at their own speed. This tunes them out of your presentation. It is a built-in distraction. If there is material that cannot be seen well on a front projection or if you have information with detail, hand that out to the audience members and briefly review it with them at one time.

- **Keep it interesting in style and content.**

Feedback Form

Your name: _____

Presenter's name: _____

What was the speaker's best quality?

Did the speaker interact with the audience? How?

What images or media did the speaker use? What did you learn from the media?

What background knowledge did you find the most helpful?

What was the most interesting idea in the presentation?

Macbeth's "If it were done" Soliloquy, Act 1, Scene 7

Group 1: If it were done when 'tis done, then 'twere well

Group 2: It were done quickly: if the assassination

Group 1: Could trammel up the consequence, and catch

Group 2: With his surcease success; that but this blow

Group 1: Might be the be-all and the end-all here,

Group 2: But here, upon this bank and shoal of time,

Group 1: We'd jump the life to come. But in these cases

Group 2: We still have judgment here; that we but teach

Group 1: Bloody instructions, which, being taught, return

Group 2: To plague the inventor: this even-handed justice

Group 1: Commends th' ingredience of our poison'd chalice

Group 2: To our own lips. He's here in double trust;

Group 1: First, as I am his kinsman and his subject,

Group 2: Strong both against the deed; then, as his host,

Group 1: Who should against his murderer shut the door,

Group 2: Not bear the knife myself. Besides, this Duncan

Group 1: Hath borne his faculties so meek, hath been

Group 2: So clear in his great office, that his virtues

Group 1: Will plead like angels, trumpet-tongued, against

Group 2: The deep damnation of his taking-off;

Group 1: And pity, like a naked new-born babe,

Group 2: Striding the blast, or heaven's cherubim, horsed

Group 1: Upon the sightless couriers of the air,

Group 2: Shall blow the horrid deed in every eye,

Group 1: That tears shall drown the wind. I have no spur

Group 2: To prick the sides of my intent, but only

Group 1: Vaulting ambition, which o'erleaps itself

Group 2: And falls on th' other—

Macbeth's "If it were done" Soliloquy, Act 1, Scene 7, Divided by Syntactical Unit

The / indicates where the line originally broke in the blank verse.

Group 1: If it were done when 'tis done,

Group 2: then 'twere well / It were done quickly:

Group 1: if the assassination / Could trammel up the consequence,

Group 2: and catch / With his surcease success;

Group 1: that but this blow / Might be the be-all and the end-all here, /

Group 2: But here,

Group 1: upon this bank and shoal of time, /

Group 2: We'd jump the life to come.

Group 1: But in these cases / We still have judgment here;

Group 2: that we but teach / Bloody instructions,

Group 1: which, being taught,

Group 2: return / To plague the inventor:

Group 1: this even-handed justice / Commends th' ingredience of our poison'd chalice / To our own lips.

Group 2: He's here in double trust; /

Group 1: First, as I am his kinsman and his subject, /

Group 2: Strong both against the deed;

Group 1: then, as his host, /

Group 2: Who should against his murderer shut the door, /

Group 1: Not bear the knife myself.

Group 2: Besides, this Duncan / Hath borne his faculties so meek,

Group 1: hath been / So clear in his great office,

Group 2: that his virtues / Will plead like angels, trumpet-tongued,

Group 1: against / The deep damnation of his taking-off; /

Group 2: And pity, like a naked new-born babe, / Striding the blast,

Group 1: or heaven's cherubim, horsed / Upon the sightless couriers of the air, /

Group 2: Shall blow the horrid deed in every eye, /

Group 1: That tears shall drown the wind.

Group 2: I have no spur / To prick the sides of my intent,

Group 1: but only / Vaulting ambition,

Group 2: which o'erleaps itself / And falls on th' other—

Macbeth's "Is this a dagger" Soliloquy, Act 2, Scene 1, for Group Recording

Groups 1, 2, and 3

Develop, rehearse, and record a dramatic reading of your lines. You can read in unison, apply different vocal techniques or emotions, or alternate readings among students.

Group 1: Is this a dagger which I see before me,
The handle toward my hand? Come, let me clutch thee.

Group 2: I have thee not, and yet I see thee still.
Art thou not, fatal vision, sensible
To feeling as to sight?

Group 3: or art thou but
A dagger of the mind, a false creation,
Proceeding from the heat-oppressed brain?

Group 4 (Audio Group)

Pick two sound effects and one song from Handout 11.4 to go with the soliloquy text. You can loop or cut any of the sounds or songs. The sound effects can go before, during, or after the speech. You can listen to the sounds on the computer. On the lines below, indicate where you would have the sounds go. Be prepared to explain your decisions.

Is this a dagger which I see before me,

The handle toward my hand? Come, let me clutch thee.

I have thee not, and yet I see thee still.

Art thou not, fatal vision, sensible

To feeling as to sight? or art thou but

A dagger of the mind, a false creation,

Proceeding from the heat-oppressed brain?

Audio Resources

File Name (all.mp3)	Length	Original File Name	Source	URL	Creative Commons License
Sound Effects					
Boiling Water	0:14	boiling bubbles ingredients.wav	Jace	http://freesound.iua.upf.edu/samplesViewSingle.php?id=19845	Sampling Plus 1.0
Crows	1:00	Craws.wav	inchadney	http://freesound.iua.upf.edu/samplesViewSingle.php?id=13735	Sampling Plus 1.0
Evil Laugh	0:08	woman_Noor_laughs_like_crow.aiff	thanvannispen	http://freesound.iua.upf.edu/samplesViewSingle.php?id=9562	Sampling Plus 1.0
Growl	0:08	growl1.wav	ubecareful	http://freesound.iua.upf.edu/samplesViewSingle.php?id=20208	Sampling Plus 1.0
Thunder	0:28	Thunder5 6-18-06.wav	Freqman	http://freesound.iua.upf.edu/samplesViewSingle.php?id=20048	Sampling Plus 1.0
Music					
Chilled Milk Music	4:29	spacehopper3_-_Chilled_Milk.mp3	Dreamsound	http://ccmixter.org/media/files/spacehopper3/6401	Attribution
Sin Q Loop Music	0:19	SinQ_Hibrid_delayedRhodes_100bpm.mp3	SinQ	http://ccmixter.org/media/files/sinq/1578	

Macbeth's "To be thus is nothing" Soliloquy, Act 3, Scene 1

To be thus is nothing;

But to be safely thus. Our fears in Banquo

Stick deep; and in his royalty of nature

Reigns that which would be fear'd: 'tis much he dares;

And, to that dauntless temper of his mind,

He hath a wisdom that doth guide his valour

To act in safety. There is none but he

Whose being I do fear: and, under him,

My Genius is rebuk'd; as, it is said,

Mark Antony's was by Caesar. He chid the sisters

When first they put the name of king upon me,

And bade them speak to him: then prophet-like

They hail'd him father to a line of kings:

Upon my head they plac'd a fruitless crown,

And put a barren sceptre in my gripe,

Thence to be wrench'd with an unlineal hand,

No son of mine succeeding. If 't be so,

For Banquo's issue have I fil'd my mind;

For them the gracious Duncan have I murder'd;

Put rancours in the vessel of my peace

Only for them; and mine eternal jewel

Given to the common enemy of man,

To make them kings, the seeds of Banquo kings!

Rather than so, come fate into the list.

And champion me to the utterance!

Macbeth's "She should have died hereafter" Soliloquy, Act 5, Scene 5

She should have died hereafter;

There would have been a time for such a word.

To-morrow, and to-morrow, and to-morrow,

Creeps in this petty pace from day to day

To the last syllable of recorded time,

And all our yesterdays have lighted fools

The way to dusty death. Out, out, brief candle!

Life's but a walking shadow, a poor player

That struts and frets his hour upon the stage

And then is heard no more: it is a tale

Told by an idiot, full of sound and fury,

Signifying nothing.

Lady Macbeth's "The raven himself" Soliloquy, Act 1, Scene 5

The raven himself is hoarse

That croaks the fatal entrance of Duncan

Under my battlements. Come, you spirits

That tend on mortal thoughts, unsex me here,

And fill me from the crown to the toe top-full

Of direst cruelty! make thick my blood;

Stop up the access and passage to remorse,

That no compunctious visitings of nature

Shake my fell purpose, nor keep peace between

The effect and it! Come to my woman's breasts,

And take my milk for gall, you murdering ministers,

Wherever in your sightless substances

You wait on nature's mischief! Come, thick night,

And pall thee in the dunnest smoke of hell,

That my keen knife see not the wound it makes,

Nor heaven peep through the blanket of the dark,

To cry "Hold, hold!"

Reflective Worksheet

Complete the following exercises. Attach additional pages as needed.

1. Describe the types of vocal techniques used (reading in unison, shouting, whispering). Include the techniques, words, and lines, and the reasons for your choice.

2. Describe the sound effects used. Include the placement of the effects and the reasons for your choice.

3. Describe the music used. Include a description of the music (including the mood it creates), when it started and ended, and three to five reasons for your choice.

4. Describe all the audio effects (echo, reverberation, pitch changes). Include the words, phrases, and lines that were affected and a description of the intended effect on the listener because of these effects.

5. List all the sound effects and music that you used.

File Name :

Length:

Original File Name:

Source *(if original, please note that)*:

URL:

Type of License (traditional or Creative Commons copyright). If original, please indicate what type of license you intend to give it, traditional or Creative Commons copyright:

Making a Scene

From Hamlet Act 1, Scenes 4 and 5

Hamlet, Horatio, and Marcellus on Stage

Horatio:
Look, my lord, it comes!

[Enter Ghost]

Hamlet:
Angels and ministers of grace defend us!
Be thou a spirit of health or goblin damn'd,
Bring with thee airs from heaven or blasts from hell,
Be thy intents wicked or charitable,
Thou comest in such a questionable shape
That I will speak to thee: I'll call thee Hamlet,
King, father, royal Dane: O, answer me!
Let me not burst in ignorance; but tell
Why thy canonized bones, hearsed in death,
Have burst their cerements; why the sepulchre,
Wherein we saw thee quietly inurn'd,
Hath oped his ponderous and marble jaws,
To cast thee up again. What may this mean,
That thou, dead corse, again in complete steel
Revisit'st thus the glimpses of the moon,
Making night hideous; and we fools of nature
So horridly to shake our disposition
With thoughts beyond the reaches of our souls?
Say, why is this? wherefore? what should we do?

[Ghost beckons Hamlet]

Horatio:
It beckons you to go away with it,
As if it some impartment did desire
To you alone.

Marcellus:
Look, with what courteous action
It waves you to a more removed ground:
But do not go with it.

Horatio:
No, by no means.

Hamlet:
It will not speak; then I will follow it.

Horatio:
Do not, my lord.

Hamlet:
Why, what should be the fear?
I do not set my life in a pin's fee;
And for my soul, what can it do to that,
Being a thing immortal as itself?
It waves me forth again: I'll follow it.

Horatio:
What if it tempt you toward the flood, my lord,
Or to the dreadful summit of the cliff
That beetles o'er his base into the sea,
And there assume some other horrible form,
Which might deprive your sovereignty of reason
And draw you into madness? think of it:
The very place puts toys of desperation,
Without more motive, into every brain
That looks so many fathoms to the sea
And hears it roar beneath.

Hamlet:
It waves me still.
Go on; I'll follow thee.

Marcellus:
You shall not go, my lord.

Hamlet:
Hold off your hands.

Horatio:
Be ruled; you shall not go.

Hamlet:
My fate cries out,
And makes each petty artery in this body
As hardy as the Nemean lion's nerve.
Still am I call'd. Unhand me, gentlemen.
By heaven, I'll make a ghost of him that lets me!
I say, away! Go on; I'll follow thee.

[Exeunt Ghost and Hamlet]

Horatio:
He waxes desperate with imagination.

Marcellus
Let's follow; 'tis not fit thus to obey him.

Horatio:
Have after. To what issue will this come?

Marcellus
Something is rotten in the state of Denmark.

Horatio:
Heaven will direct it.

Marcellus
Nay, let's follow him

[Exeunt Marcellus and Horatio]

Enter Ghost and Hamlet

Hamlet
Where wilt thou lead me? speak; I'll go no further.

Ghost:
Mark me.

Hamlet:
I will.

Ghost:
My hour is almost come,
When I to sulphurous and tormenting flames
Must render up myself.

Hamlet:
Alas, poor ghost!

Ghost:
Pity me not, but lend thy serious hearing
To what I shall unfold.

Hamlet:
Speak; I am bound to hear.

Ghost:
So art thou to revenge, when thou shalt hear.

Hamlet:
What?

Ghost:
I am thy father's spirit,
Doom'd for a certain term to walk the night,
And for the day confined to fast in fires,
Till the foul crimes done in my days of nature
Are burnt and purged away. But that I am forbid
To tell the secrets of my prison-house,
I could a tale unfold whose lightest word
Would harrow up thy soul, freeze thy young blood,
Make thy two eyes, like stars, start from their spheres,
Thy knotted and combined locks to part
And each particular hair to stand on end,
Like quills upon the fretful porpentine:
But this eternal blazon must not be
To ears of flesh and blood. List, list, O, list!
If thou didst ever thy dear father love—

Hamlet:
O God!

Ghost:
Revenge his foul and most unnatural murder.

Group Analysis

In groups, view the scene and answer the following questions.

People (actors and costumes)

- What are the actors doing who are speaking?

- What is their emotional state?

- How can you tell?

- Does this state change over time?

- What are the actors doing who are not speaking?

- Are any lines cut? Are any added?

Sounds (music and sound effects)

- How would you describe the music?

- When does the music play?

- Does it change?

- What are the sound effects?

Things (set and props)

- What is the location?

- How is the location important to the action of the scene?

- How does the director portray this location? Is it dark? Is it light?

- List five adjectives that would describe this setting.

- What props are used?

- What are the costumes of each person in the scene?

Camera (angles and editing)

- What does the camera focus on?

- Are their any close-ups? When, of what?

- Does the camera move?

- If the camera was the point of view of a person, who would it be?

- Does this point of view change? When?

- Do the scenes speed up or jump quickly at any time? When?

Digital Storytelling

In a group of four, enact one of the following sets of lines.

Find images related to your scene on the Web—castles, ghosts, paintings of this scene from Hamlet. You can do a Web search or go to Hamlet on the Ramparts (http://shea.mit.edu/ramparts/collections/art/index.htm), which offers more than 100 digital images of famous paintings of this scene alone.

Enact this scene and take digital photographs of your group members in action. You can stage close-ups and freeze the action for a better image. Your final production will be a digital story. You will be able to arrange, zoom, crop, pan, and transition all images. You will add music, sound effects, and the spoken lines of your group.

Set 1

Horatio:
Look, my lord, it comes!

[Enter Ghost]

Hamlet:
Angels and ministers of grace defend us!
Be thou a spirit of health or goblin damn'd

Set 2

Horatio:
It beckons you to go away with it,
As if it some impartment did desire
To you alone.

Marcellus:
Look, with what courteous action
It waves you to a more removed ground:
But do not go with it.

Set 3

Hamlet:
It will not speak; then I will follow it.

Horatio:
Do not, my lord.

Set 4

Hamlet:
Why, what should be the fear?
I do not set my life in a pin's fee;

Horatio:
What if it tempt you toward the flood, my lord,
Or to the dreadful summit of the cliff

Set 5

Hamlet:
It waves me still.
Go on; I'll follow thee.

Marcellus:
You shall not go, my lord.

Hamlet:
Hold off your hands.

Set 6

Horatio:
Be ruled; you shall not go.

Hamlet:
My fate cries out,
And makes each petty artery in this body
As hardy as the Nemean lion's nerve.

Storyboard Outline

Organize the content and order of your material using the chart on the following page. For images, you can list ones that you have or will be getting. Your narration can apply to one image or go across several. You can also have images without narration. Please remember that this storyboard will be a starting point. You will change your content and organization as you develop your work on the computer.

Name _____ page _____ of _____ *(copy as needed)*

Audio Effect and Music:				
Images				
Narration				
Notes:				
Teacher Comments:				

Index

Page references followed by f indicate figures.

A

activities
   Audio Interviews for Perspective and
      Analysis unit, 98–99
   Blogging and Independent Reading Projects
      unit, 67–69
   A Document in Madness unit, 92–94
   Hamlet's Ghosts unit, 155–156
   iBard unit, 146–149
   Memoirs and Online Peer Editing unit,
      83–87
   performance-based, 155–156
   Persuasive Communication unit, 107–109
   Podcourse unit, 43–46
   The Power of a Person Making a Point unit,
      140–141
   Teaching with Fanfiction unit, 54–62
   Technology and the Research Paper unit,
      124–132
   Wikis unit, 76–79
"Agreement on Guidelines for Classroom
   Copying in Not-for-Profit Educational
   Institutions with Respect to Books and
   Periodicals," 24
All the Web, 161
Altavista, 161
Amazon.com Listmania lists, 67
American Library Association, 24
anchored learning, 103–111
anticopying technologies, 24–25
articulation
   rubric for audio essays, 46
   rubric for persuasive communication, 110
assessment. See also rubrics
   authentic, 103–111
Association of Research Libraries, 24

Audacity, 159
   Podcourse applications, 39, 43
   resources for, 163
   resources for teachers, 41
   vocal recordings of soliloquies, 147, 148f
audio
   anticopying technologies, 25
   Audio Interviews for Perspective and
      Analysis unit, 95–101
   digital, 160
   editing, 143–150
   essay assignments, 173
   formats, 160–161
   iBard unit, 143–150
   interview scripts, 99
   peer responses to audio essays, 174
   Podcourse unit, 39–47
   recording interviews, 99
   resources for, 163–164
   resources for audio interviews, 97
   resources related to copyleft, 163
   rubric for audio effects, 149
   rubric for audio essays, 46
   rubric for audio interviews, 100
   rubric for coordination of images, narration,
      and audio, 111
   rubric for listener responses, 101
   rubric for mastering soliloquies through
      performance and editing audio, 149
   rubric for use of music and other audio, 111
   sample interviews for models and discussion,
      97
   sources of, 161–162
   transferring from CDs to computers, 163
   turning audio files into podcasts with
      Blogger, 43
   using, 159–163